Seagulls Don t Lie!

B. Lee McDowell

B. Lee McDowell

SEAGULLS DON'T LIE!
Copyright © 2020 by B. Lee McDowell
Published by Dowadad Press
A division of Lee McDowell Christian Ministries, Inc.
P.O. Box 633244, Nacogdoches, TX 75963
leemccm.wixsite.com/lmcm

ISBN: 979-8-6124499-5-9

All scripture quotations are taken from the King James Version of the Bible

Cover photo by Will Drost, www.willdrost.photoshelter.com
Printed in the United States of America

B. Lee McDowell
Lee McDowell Christian Ministries
P. O. Box 633244, Nacogdoches, TX
75963 936-645-9091
leemccm.wixsite.com/lmcm

I dedicate this book to my loving and supportive wife, Barbara, who has stood by my side these past 51 years as our life took twists and turns, ups and downs, highs and lows, and she has been all that God wanted me to have as a wife, "a help-meet," re: Genesis 2:18.

I also dedicate this book to our wonderful and gifted daughters, Kelly and Jennifer.
These two are truly "an heritage of the LORD: and the fruit of the womb is His reward."
Psalm 127:3

Acknowledgments

This book didn't just happen. An idea came about one day, after a most unusual fishing experience with my saltwater mentor and much more my great friend of so many years, Capt. Bruce Baugh. His words are the seed that were planted in my heart around 30 years ago. They took root and grew, and finally the fruit of its great truth resulted in the pages you will explore. *Seagulls Don't Lie!* is a compilation of Truths that my God has given me through many faithful teachers and mentors. These are contributions from family, friends, and fellow ministers for which I am deeply grateful. Each has had a dramatic impact in my life. I regard these Truths as the revelations of God's grace to me.

My appreciation first is to God for dramatically saving my physical life more than once to allow me to continue on the journey He planned for me and allowing me to write down the things in this book (and hopefully a few others to follow). I also must mention my appreciation for God giving me His Life in my New Birth, insuring my ultimate spending of eternity with Him. And with the gift of His Soul, I have His Mind, His Emotions, and His Will to enjoy His Life Lived out in my earthsuit. I haven't received all revelation from His Mind, but I am most grateful for what I have been given right now.

Second, for over 51 years I have loved and enjoyed my bride, Barbara, by my side and as my companion in this beautiful journey God has given us. She is the perfect "help-meet" as Moses shared God's words in Genesis 2:18. Barbara has been by me every step of the way. We have learned the Truths presented in this book together. God deepens my love and appreciation for her every day.

Next, I am grateful for our two daughters, Kelly and Jennifer, that God gave Barbara and me. They have been the apple of this father's eye. I love them very much and am very proud of them. In the realm of things that our family has been through in pastoral life, I am grateful God has sustained their love for Him. They have been a sounding board over the years for virtually all the Truths presented herein. And I am grateful for our two sons-in-law, Chad and Braxton, and our four grandkids, Darby, Braden, Garrett, and Ashleigh. Our family is a demonstration of Grace and Truth shared and believed.

Every author has those to whom He owes much. Pastor John D. Morgan, Sagemont Church, Houston, Texas, is the one whom God Lived through to bring myself and Barbara to our Lord Jesus Christ.

His sermon, "Ye Must Be Born Again," on May 18, 1980 (actually at the very moments Mt. St. Helens was blowing!), dramatically changed our lives and that of generations to come. Acknowledgment and gratefulness seem too little to speak of what we think and appreciate about Pastor John Morgan and the great Sagemont Church.

My appreciation goes to the many individuals mentioned in this book as mentors, teachers, and friends. They have been the earthsuits God spoke and wrote through to bring His tremendous revelations. God does that. Each has been blessed in their own way with God Living through them.

I am especially thankful for two friends, Rick and Abby West, who have gotten as excited about this book coming to fruition as I have been all along in writing and anticipating it being in print. Rick and Abby have each written books. They knew the process of finally holding in their hands the printed version of the thoughts and words in their minds. Their encouragement and guidance in the process of getting this to print has been invaluable.

I am grateful for Will Drost, a good friend of Capt. Bruce Baugh. Will has opened his vast reservoir of saltwater photos to give me a choice of seagull pictures for a terrific picture for the front cover. Will is a great fisherman and expert photographer. You can catch Will's awesome photos at www.willdrost.photoshelter.com. He also expresses tremendous respect for Capt. Baugh. Will speaks of the first time he met Bruce his thought was about catching big speckled trout, but the truth was it didn't compare to Bruce's knowledge and continued success. But, most importantly, Will says, Bruce is a gentleman, a great person to be around. I totally agree.

Finally, my deepest gratitude goes to my Lord Jesus Christ. He is my very Life. And I pray that You, Lord Jesus, receive any praise for any good that may come from this book. As You have said, "...for without Me, ye can do nothing." I acknowledge that for sure! May His Love and Truth be revealed to every person who reads this book.

Well, amen.

Contents

Foreword by Dr. John D. Morgan

It was Sunday morning, May 18, 1980, and God was present at Sagemont Church in Houston, Texas. The building was a gymnasium being used as a worship facility where the simple gospel message was being presented. With a basketball goal over my head as I preached, I feared that if I made a powerful statement, someone might shout "Two" instead of "Amen." A seeking couple sat in front of me. They were beautiful in appearance, compassionate in spirit, and successful in business but lacking in their personal relationship with Jesus Christ. That morning, God brought Lee and Barbara out of darkness into His glorious light.

Awakened to a desperate spiritual state, they called the church on Monday morning and talked with my secretary, Beverly Chambers, who made an appointment for them to see me Tuesday morning. In my office after further discussion both Lee and Barbara placed their trust in Jesus Christ to be their Savior. They were "born again" and the following Sunday morning they came forward at the invitation in the morning service to publicly profess their faith in Christ. That Sunday evening they were baptized by immersion, symbolizing the death, burial and resurrection of Jesus Christ and picturing their spiritual death and being raised to a new life. Their two beautiful daughters saw an immediate change in their mom and dad. They too would soon follow in their parent's steps of obedience to Christ.

It has been my privilege and joy to see the testimony of 2 Timothy 2:2 played out in this family's lives. Having received truth on May 18, 1980, then passing truth on to other faithful saints who also pass truth forward. *Seagulls Don't Lie!* will bless you as you read their testimony. Untold numbers of people have come to know and follow Christ because they saw and heard the truth "You must be born again!"

Read *Seagulls Don't Lie!* and be prepared to hear a story that can change your life forever. Just think of what God can and will do when one family comes to salvation through Christ, and then begins to share His truth with others. All the time receiving more truth and sharing all with so many. And remember, "You must be born again!"

Dr. John D. Morgan, Pastor
Sagemont Church
Houston, Texas

Lee McDowell Christian Ministries

B. Lee McDowell, Author

there is nothing the presence of Christ cannot overcome

All books by B. Lee McDowell are available in Nacogdoches, and online @ Amazon/Kindle

preaching or teaching engagements are calendared on *love offering* basis

eGroups (via email) to study books in depth

to sign up for eGroups or LMCM Mailing List, contact us...

1737 CR 2051   Nacogdoches, TX 75965

Phone: 936-559-5696   email: leemccm@gmail.com

blog: www.leemccmviews.blogspot.com

website: www.leemccm.wixsite.com/lmcm

author's page: www.amazon/com/~/e/B083LQXJZ4

Preface by Capt. Bruce Baugh

Seagulls Don't Lie! is a book about Truth. And with great joy I was able to introduce my pastor, Lee McDowell, to my passion of saltwater fishing, and the great truth that seagulls never lie to fishermen: there are always trout or redfish in the water chasing bait underneath seagulls circling above.

I first met Lee when he came to visit me after my wife had visited the church he pastored. We had a mutual love for fishing. And he shared with me the greatest truth in life, that being a 'good person' would not get me to heaven, but really realizing the truth of Jesus Christ paying for my sins and trusting in Him as my Savior, I could be Born Again becoming a Christian. Lee baptized me soon after I trusted Christ as my Savior.

Lee and I have since spent many days and hours on the water together, chasing the birds and otherwise! And I am more than excited that my beloved seagulls have become the catalyst for such a great book expounding on many spiritual truths that my Savior has given to give life to those who believe.

The truth shall make you free. Thank You, Lord!

Capt. Bruce Baugh, Fishing Guide
Tide Line Charters, Lake Calcasieu, LA
337-660-1814

Introduction

"Ever so often in life an extraordinary relationship unfolds in a most unexpected place…" (David L. Cook, *Golf's Sacred Journey*, p. 35)

My life has had several of those relationships unfold since becoming a part of the Family of God. This book is about how more than 30 folks (family, friends, some acquaintances, some pastors, some bible teachers, some evangelists, and some missionaries) have brought life-changing Truths to my life. These are life-changing Truths due to their Spiritual origination and content. There actually have been MANY MORE such people, and many more such Truths God has brought my way, but these stand out as special folks for special reasons. I do ask God to bless the ones I don't mention in this book! And, in the process of compiling the book, I have included several as "others" and "faithful ones" that God brought to me. Praise the LORD for each and every one!

The title *Seagulls Don't Lie!* is about TRUTH. It is about that type of bird known to those on the coasts of the world, when put into the realm of the fisherman gives an awareness of the difference in Truth or a lie. Seagulls never lie to the fisherman. TRUTH never lies to humans. TRUTH MAKES US FREE. The big question for us is "are we chasing a lie, or chasing Truth?" Are we pursuing what looks like "the truth," but isn't. Jesus Is The Way, The Truth, and The Life; everything else is not The Way, The Truth, or The Life.

So in essence, this book is about JESUS. Truth is found in only one place: JESUS. TRUTH is a Person, the Lord Jesus Christ. John 14:6, "I am the truth," Jesus declared to Thomas, the one who is known as "the doubter." Lies are found in only one place: Satan. In John 8:44, Jesus made clear to the Jews who wouldn't believe Him who was/is their "father":

> "Ye are of your father the devil, and the lusts of your father ye will do. He was a murderer from the beginning, and abode not in the truth, because there is no truth in him. When he speaketh a lie, he speaketh of his own: for he is a liar, and the father of it."

I like to ask one simple question if I ever am wondering if someone is speaking Truth to me: "Will that stand as TRUTH before the Throne of the Lord Jesus Christ?"

I can't recall just exactly when God began urging me to consider writing of my journey down this road. My life began back on June 1,

1945, in the small Texas town of Commerce. Back then, population around 5,000. Born in Allen Hospital, which was in the front of the home of Dr. and Mrs. Allen on Live Oak street. Bill and Beth McDowell, the proud parents. O. B. and Mildred Bradford, and Maurine McDowell, proud grandparents. Even at the age of 3, God intervened in a mighty way to keep me on the path He had planned. My appendix ruptured, and Dr. Allen pronounced me dead after working to save me. But his wife and nurse, Coy, (who was a great friend of my grandparents and parents) kept "working with me" and guess what: she supposedly brought me back to life. Well, I did have life. People might discuss or argue about the truth of the result of her actions, but I do know this truth: I lived on.

Around midnight on March 16, 2003, I suffered a heart attack. Only by the grace of God and His working in the events that followed did I make it out of our home alive. And then to be transferred later the next morning from one hospital to another to be treated by Dr. Antoine Younis at St. Luke's Hospital in the Houston Medical Center was a gift from God. I did contract the deadly MRSA staph infection after another doctor inserted a defibrillator into my body, but God graciously spared my life once more. Twice in one month I had come within seconds of physically dying. Christ's Life in my earthsuit was not finished.

All through the 73 physical years God has given me so far, I have seen and received Truth that has made a great difference in my life, and the lives of family, friends, and others that God Himself was responsible for me being exposed to. The idea of my writing a book actually began as a thought of "Grandpa's Goodies For His Grandkids" (another book I am working on at present). I had the desire to write down many Truths that I could pass on to family. (I can't tell you how many times I heard folks at a funeral or "viewing," or visiting in a family's home, say, "I wish Dad -or, Mom, Grandpa, Grandma- would have written down all the things he/she did in their life, all the things they knew about (whatever)" etc.). This book is my joy of writing down and presenting some of those "extraordinary fellowships" and "life-changing Truths" God has blessed me with.

You will meet folks who are just like you and me, people on the life-journey God has put them on. But, along life's way, each has impacted me in a most profound way and manner. In the extended, individual stories section (chapters 1-14) you will meet:

Bruce Baugh – a fireman by calling, a fishing friend with a giving heart

John Morgan – a pastor by calling, with an encouraging shepherd/ evangelist's heart

Bill McDowell – a teacher/coach/counselor by calling, my father with a warm heart for his son

O. B. Bradford – a teacher by calling, my grandfather with a caring heart for his grandson

Bill Hinson – an educator by calling, an older family friend with a teaching heart

Bill Shelton – a professional golfer by calling, a father-figure and genuine encourager by heart

Michael Wells – a missionary by calling, a teacher of Christ's Life with an intense sharing heart

Gary & Anne Marie Ezzo – a bible teaching couple by calling, loving encouragers by heart

Charles Stanley – a pastor/teacher by calling, with a shepherd/ pastor of pastors heart

Bruce Wilkinson – a bible expositor by calling, an encourager and truth sharer in heart

Bill Gothard - a bible teacher by calling, with a great personal discipleship heart

Bill Sevier – an engineer by calling, a faithful servant of God and friend by heart

Travis B. Bryan, Jr. – a banker by calling, an encourager with the great heart of Christ

In chapters 15 and 16, you will meet and get a glimpse of "others" who have given me some of the greatest truths and applications of the Christ Life that have had a dramatic impact in my life, along with some "fruit," folks whom God allowed me to share with the truths I gleaned from all of the above, but now give testimony of how it was passed on "from faith to faith." In chapter 17, I close with some personal notes about my journey.

You will notice that I capitalize the "T" in Truth most of the time in this book. When it comes to a Truth of God, I believe it is Him and He deserves a capital T. Likewise, you will notice that I capitalize the "L" in Life most of the time. When it comes to talking about Life in Christ, I am speaking of His Life. And His Life deserves a capital L. There are also sometimes where I highlight particular words or phrases in scripture quotations by putting them into bold print or underline or caps. Sometimes, I may note such, others I may not. The words in the Bible are never in bold print.

What an incredible JOY to re-think, re-live, and rejoice in the numerous, tremendous, incredulous stories of God's TRUTHS being shared with little ole ME over 73 years of life He has given me so far. Well, amen. May they bring some joy to you, and stir you to perhaps share with your loved ones, friends, and who knows whom the similar timeless TRUTHS God has given you.

B. Lee McDowell

About the Author

Born into a family of educators, Lee McDowell instead set his sights on other fields and first became a professional golfer before settling into a lucrative sales career. But God had different plans.

With a father who was a college tennis player and later a multi-sport coach, Lee was involved in athletics from an early age. An injury at age 12 changed his athletic plans, and he turned to golf, playing on the Texas A&M University Golf Team, ultimately winning the Texas State Amateur Golf Championship, and playing on the PGA Tour for a couple of years.

In his late twenties, he became a salesman where he worked his way up to become a manager/vice-president of the world's largest small-boat dealership, Louis DelHomme Marine in Houston, Texas.

But in 1981, God called Lee to a life of ministry. He studied at Southwestern Baptist Theological Seminary, and began his life's calling. Having been a minister in various forms in various towns for over 30 years, his extensive experiences and acquaintances have given him a broad perspective of Life as a Christian which show forth in his writings.

Life changed in 2003 when Lee suffered a major heart attack. God then had him serving in part-time pastoral roles until his 70th birthday. At that point, God moved Lee into writing books and blogs. And from an encounter 20 years before at a men's retreat where he got the idea of doing ministry at a local park on Sunday mornings, Lee has been leading his ministry "Christ In The Park" in Nacogdoches for over 3 years now.

B. Lee McDowell is the president of Lee McDowell Christian Ministries, a preaching, teaching, discipleship-making ministry.

Lee and his wife of 51 years, Barbara, have 2 children and 4 grandchildren.

B. Lee McDowell
Lee McDowell Christian Ministries
P.O. Box 633244, Nacogdoches, TX 75963
936-645-9091
leemccm.wixsite.com/lmcm

Chapter One

Bruce Baugh – "The Birds Are Working!"

"And ye shall know the truth, and the truth shall make you free."
John 8:32

A fellow named Bruce Baugh has taught me almost everything I know about salt-water fishing for speckled trout, redfish, and flounder. He is an expert. He has an incredible knack for knowing the water, the fish, the correct bait, and the "bite." Bruce also has a great heart for sharing what he knows. He is a wonderful friend, characterized by so many of the Life traits that our Lord Jesus Christ gave us examples of. And interestingly, God used Bruce to plant a seed for the idea, inspiration, and motivation to compile this book.

It was way back in the late 1980's that I first met Bruce Baugh. He was a Houston, Texas, fireman at station #57 working 24 hour shifts on the days his schedule prescribed. Bruce also had a part-time job working as a security man at Foley's department store on days when he wasn't at the fire station. He had a third "job"…that of salt-water angler. We could call it a job since Bruce worked as hard as anyone could to become as knowledgeable, proficient, and successful in this line of "work" as anyone ever did in any other profession. It was a natural thing for him to do. He started off as a young boy in southern Louisiana loving the saltwater. And here we are 30 years later and Bruce is a professional salt-water fishing guide in those same waters of Cajun-land.

But I didn't meet Bruce at any of those three places. It wasn't a "chance" meeting. It wasn't a meeting by "luck." It was a divine appointment. His wife then had attended church one Sunday morning where I was the pastor. As Barbara and the girls and I headed to our car after the service, a young lady was at her car next to ours. I didn't recognize her, so I spoke out to introduce us. After a couple of questions about her, I asked if she was married. She teared up. Her husband, she said, didn't attend church. Within a couple of minutes, she mentioned something about him also being a fisherman. I really can't remember if she said he was a fireman first, or a fisherman first. Anyhow, I jumped at the chance to go meet this fisherman. And from that first encounter with Bruce, we have been best of friends ever since.

We are natural friends for two reasons: brothers in Christ, and lovers of fishing. I have learned so much from this man about rods, reels, line, tying knots, baits, tides, water conditions…and about birds. Especially seagulls!

Some people like to talk about looking for "slicks" when bay fishing, but give me the "seagulls" every time!

I remember the day just like it was yesterday, even though that was 30 years ago! My salt-water fishing mentor was all excited as we raced across East Matagorda Bay toward the Oyster Farm, a shell reef on the southern shoreline. Bruce's 17-ft. Mako with an 85hp Yamaha "screamed" into the incredibly beautiful dawning hour. There is nothing like the thrill of anticipation as the spray off the boat bouncing over waves and cutting into the salty water flies into your face as you fly toward that first fishing spot! (45mph in a 17' boat is a lot like "flying"!). And, I was getting excited over Bruce's excitement! Billy, a professional guide friend, had told Bruce the trout were really biting early on the shell reefs and "under the birds" in late morning. Bruce had not said much about the "birds" as we left his house and headed down south, but it would become the topic of the day before noon!

We headed toward the Oyster Farm shell reef area, a wonderful conglomeration of small shell reefs, and caught some nice typical "Matagorda trout" (about 2+ pounds, on average; larger than those in other bays closest to Houston; probably due to the lesser pressure from fishermen, many fewer anglers on any given day). But the action wasn't as fast that morning as Bruce would have liked. As we eased away from the reefs and started up on a plane heading to the west…suddenly, Bruce shouted, "Birds! Lee, look toward the north shoreline!" My eyes back then did not focus on objects too well at great distances (hoooo-boy! Are they different these days! I will tell you about that in a moment.). Eventually I saw them. There must have been 50 of them…SEAGULLS! We could hear the squawking almost before I could focus well and see them. They were circling and diving…straight into the water. I really didn't know what I was in for!

Bruce started shouting instructions: "When we get close, we will kill the motor. I will get on the front deck, lower the troll motor, and we will ease our way toward that water that is disturbed under the birds. There will be trout or redfish taking our bait almost every cast!" I almost couldn't believe what I was hearing. Catch a fish almost every cast???

20

Bruce expertly stopped the Yamaha a measured distance from the birds. We were where the wind could assist in moving us toward the group with ease in addition to the troll motor. Then he grabbed his rod and leapt onto the front deck (quite an agile man!), lowered the troll motor, and cast in between the circling birds. DON'T SCARE THE BIRDS! I immediately grabbed my rod and climbed onto the rear deck. In what seemed like less than 10 seconds, we had cast out among the seagulls, saw shrimp jumping out of the water as the trout chased them, and quickly had two trout hung & headed to the boat! "I'm ON!," Bruce exclaimed. Then ME! WOW! This is exciting! I learned a great lesson right then: *Seagulls Don't Lie!* That's truth. Think about it. ALWAYS, TRUTH NEVER LIES. The TRUTH really does "make you free." Think about it. Jesus IS the Truth (John 14:6). He cannot lie. Jesus really will make you free! (John 8:32, 36).

"Seagulls don't lie!" Seagulls don't lie??? What did he mean? Later when the fish stopped chasing the shrimp and the seagulls disappeared as quickly as they first appeared, I asked. Bruce started telling me about these other birds in the bays, calling them Liar Birds. Their real name is terns. They are a strikingly similar bird to the seagulls, like a counterfeit gull. Almost the same color, but about 2/3 the size of gulls. Takes a close look to distinguish the two apart, especially from 100 yards or more while they are circling and diving into the water. Thing is, these Liar Birds act like the seagulls, but they NEVER are present and diving down when the trout are chasing shrimp. The Liar Birds are ALWAYS after trash fish and "stuff" in the water. Liars. Liars are just plain and simply liars. God tells us that satan is the father of all lies, because there is no Truth in him (John 8:44).

BUT, now listen. Bruce continued his explanation. When there are speckled trout or redfish chasing shrimp and driving them to the top of the water, the seagulls know that truth, and will almost immediately (from who knows where they have been!) descend out of the sky and start circling and diving down to feed on the shrimp. And anglers with any idea of what is happening will get to that spot lightning fast and cast deftly into the boiling water (careful not to hang one of the seagulls darting around), and eagerly wait for that tug of the trout or redfish on the end of the line. The truth is: Diving seagulls MAKE you catch trout or redfish. Many times since that first day in East Matagorda Bay, I have heard Bruce exclaim: "The birds are working!" Four words. Four words that have forever changed my hopes of catching a limit of speckled trout or redfish. Never has a truth made any fisherman free so much (free of false information, free of the wrong ideas that don't work or bring desired results, free of fellowship with anyone who will steer you in the wrong way) when it comes to fishing for speckled trout than these beautiful words coming out of the mouth of a knowledgeable saltwater angler. From the day of learning that truth, I never go saltwater fishing without casting my eyes constantly toward the horizon in all directions, longing for that truth that will make my day. I have also found out in all aspects of life, God's Truth will make my day. God's Truth has always made me FREE from all the false information, all the wrong ideas that don't work or bring desired results, all the fellowship with anyone who would steer me in the wrong way – or, won't stand for the Truths of God.

I love wade fishing in the shallow waters of the Gulf Coast. From the moments before the first glimpse of light on the Eastern horizon to the moments when the only way to get to the bank (or back to the boat!) is to just know where you're heading due to darkness coming upon you. I love being IN the water, moving around, searching for that smallest indication that there is bait, and usually game fish, right there in front of you. Those crazy speckled trout travel in groups and travel a lot looking for bait fish, usually mullet. But at those times of the year when shrimp are in the shallow bays, trout fishermen go crazy as the birds start working.

So never forget this: the trout are going after the shrimp, the shrimp make their way to the surface of the water trying to escape the trout, the birds (with eyes that can see more than we can ever imagine) spot the shrimp breaking the water AND FROM OUT OF NOWHERE flocks of seagulls swoop down to catch a shrimp…diving down and grasping a jumping shrimp. Maybe there will be 15 seagulls, maybe there will be 50 gulls (we've seen as many as 150 or more!), but make no mistake about it the seagulls know the moment. If the fish stop chasing the shrimp at any moment, the seagulls will drop down and lazily sit on the water. Then one or two nervously rise up and fly around "looking." Then back down to sit on the water. Then rising up and swooping around and around until that moment there is the spotting of shrimp beneath the surface of the water, or some starting to break the surface. At that, the gulls all rise and start squawking, circling, then diving down to grab the prey.

The truth of trout or redfish chasing the shrimp to the water's surface generates another truth, seagulls swarming and diving for the shrimp, which leads the fisherman to KNOW there are trout or redfish in the vicinity of that boiling water. ALWAYS! Seagulls never lie! TRUTH cannot lie.

Let's get back to those 4 words, "The birds are working!" Bruce and I have been wade fishing many times. It doesn't matter how many fish we have caught, but when Bruce screams out those four words, immediately he has us heading back to the boat, quickly getting the anchor up, and revving the motor to head straight toward this now visible group of birds circling and diving down into the water. All he can say as we make our way about ½ mile or so to the birds is: "The birds are working!" He is like a broken record. "The birds are working! The birds are working! The birds are working!"

Several years later (May, 1999) I was with a friend, Ricky Grunden, and three of his boys, Hunter, Ricky, Jr., and Kenneth. We were down at Crystal Beach near Galveston, staying at the family beach shack (my in-laws, Charlie and Rosemary Becka, had this place on the Bolivar Peninsula near Galveston). In fact, Bruce had loaned us his boat to use for two or three days fishing in East Galveston Bay. The weather was perfect for doing some wade fishing.

One morning I had gotten the guys up before daylight, fixed breakfast, then we launched at Stingaree Marina and headed toward the NE shoreline at the Anahuac National Wildlife Refuge. It is an area Bruce had taken me to several times that produced good trout fishing. I had mentioned to the boys about the "seagull thing" somewhere along the way. It was just after daylight. The sun was coming up in our face. What a terrific sight as that orange globe peeked over the horizon!

We anchored about 20 yards from the shoreline, slipped into the water, and were casting and moving slowly around trying to locate some fish. I don't remember us being there very long before one of the boys says, "Mr. Lee, is that the birds working out there?" I turned away from the shoreline where I had been headed and looked out toward the middle of the bay. By golly, there were about 25 seagulls circling and diving about 500 yards from our boat! "Get in the boat! Get in the boat!" I exclaimed. We got in, turned the motor on, and headed to an upwind position. Within a few minutes the guys were all experiencing "*Seagulls Don't Lie!*" What a fun time for the boys. What another show of truth.

Well, that family and I experienced many more interesting and exciting moments while at the beach shack, including a trip to a Galveston hospital for treatment of a dog-bite to Kenneth at a marina. But I know those guys will not soon forget the day we saw "the birds working."

Here's another example. Several years later, Bruce had moved to Lake Calcasieu just south of Lake Charles. He and his wife Carol have a great place, including a double-wide trailer for fishermen to spend the night before heading out before daylight the next morning on a guided fishing trip. Bruce has a well-known and well-respected guide service (see end of chapter for complete info). Bruce let me bring some friends.

Getting up well before daylight, we loaded up and drove west from Bruce's place. Turning south off I-10, we headed to a launch that took us to Sabine Lake. On the way over, I had asked Bruce to explain to my friends about the seagulls. Same story, umpteenth verse...lol! Bruce started by telling them about these other birds in the bays, calling them Liar Birds. He said "their real name is terns. They are a strikingly similar bird to the seagulls, like a counterfeit gull. Almost the same color, but about 2/3 the size of gulls. Takes a close look to distinguish the two apart, especially from 100 yards or more while they are circling and diving into the water. Thing is, these Liar Birds act like the seagulls, but they NEVER are present and diving down when the trout are chasing shrimp. The Liar Birds are always after trash fish and 'stuff' in the water. BUT... when there are seagulls flying around, circling and diving down into the water, you can know that there are trout or redfish chasing shrimp, and the shrimp jumping out of the water to get away from the fish chasing them is what has brought the seagulls in the first place. Seagulls never lie! The seagulls have been working lately. It is that time of the year. Fishing should be great!"

We had barely arrived at the north end of the lake when we spotted so many seagulls we couldn't count them! We made our approach on the upwind side of where the birds were. The breeze of the 5-10mph wind drifted our boat toward the scene. With rods in hand, Bruce on the front deck, me in the back of the boat, my friends in between, we anxiously awaited the second we could cast out to the disturbed water that we knew probably held a great number of speckled trout, and perhaps some redfish, working under the shrimp causing the water to be unsettled, and particularly causing the seagulls to be circling and diving down to grab some shrimp. That first cast. A couple of turns on the reel. It wasn't long until the next sweetest words sounded out, "I'm on!" Bruce had hung a trout. Then I hollered out, "I'm on!" Pretty soon all of us were catching a fish at the same time! We didn't take the time to put them on ice in the cooler. We quickly threw them onto the deck of the boat and cast our bait back into the water. "I'm on!!!" Then again, then again, then again... then all of a sudden...nothing. Some of the seagulls disappeared into the clear sky to where we couldn't spot them. The others landed on the water, just sitting there like nothing is going on. The water went relatively still again. No bait jumping, no fish grabbing our bait. Nothing. It was like a light switch had been turned off. But within just a few moments we had caught 4 or 5 fish each. Wow! This is fishing! No…it's "catching"! This is it!

Bruce started putting the trout lying on the floor of the boat into the ice chest just in front of the center console. It was beautiful. Speckled trout are beautiful. The black spots all over the silvery sides of the fish with a purple-hued back-drop make the speckled trout one of the most beautiful fish you could ever hold in your hands. Of course the anticipation of the non-fishy tasting, great-flaked fish filets fried up in cornmeal along with some cole-slaw, French fries, and hush-puppies (my good friend, Jim Adams, in Nacogdoches, calls them "shut-up dogs." Of course, he's East Texas all the way!) Hoooooo-boy! What a meal!

OK. Let's get back to the boat. As we finished gathering the trout off the floor of the boat and putting them into the cooler, here came the golden words off Bruce's lips once more: "*Seagulls don't lie!*" When the fishing ended a couple of hours later after chasing a few more groups of circling seagulls, we had caught 5 limits of trout and a few redfish. TRUTH KNOWS THE WAY!

Here's another great truth: TRUTH never changes. TRUTH cannot change. No need to remember what you have said before when you start talking about a specific truth, the story will remain the same. Life is like that. Truth brings Life (Jesus' Life) to any situation.

But have you noticed, liars have to keep up with their stories. Lies change from one minute to the next, and liars usually have to keep telling another lie to cover the error of the previous lie. Lies are deceitful. Lies bring emptiness and false hope. Those dang terns always let you down when you discover it is them! It is never that way with TRUTH!

So, listen! When there are speckled trout chasing shrimp and driving them to the top of the water, the seagulls will descend out of the sky and start diving down to feed on the shrimp. And seasoned saltwater anglers will get to that spot lightning fast and cast deftly into the boiling water (careful not to hang one of the seagulls darting around), and anxiously wait for that tug of the trout on the end of the line. It's a sure thing. And, WHEN GOD TELLS YOU SOMETHING, any person knowing God will cling to that Truth and know that God will just as surely establish His faith in you so that no one can talk you out of believing Him!

I have limited out on speckled trout under the seagulls in East Matagorda Bay (one Fall Bruce and I went fishing 10 times in this bay… each time each of us limiting out on speckled trout…mostly because of the seagulls), West Matagorda Bay, East Galveston Bay, Trinity Bay, Sabine Lake, and Lake Calcasieu…which gives Christians another major thought to remember and act upon: God's Truth, just as the truth of the seagulls, will work wherever you are and whenever you need it.

How could saltwater fishing get any better than that? Every angler wants to catch fish. Every die hard angler wants to catch a limit of fish for a given species. Every fisherman with any sort of heart for wanting to know HOW to catch a limit wants to know any and all TRUTHS that will end with a stringer full of fish for the day. HOW CAN LIFE get any better than having TRUTH in your life!?!

Now, listen. The whole point of this book hinges on a great Truth God has told us clearly: "The TRUTH shall MAKE you free." As a fisherman at heart, I like to say, "The truth has me HOOKED!" A fisherman without the truth of how to catch a fish is like a human living in bondage to some sort of sin or lie. There is no fun in the water. A fisherman with the truth of "*Seagulls don't lie!*" is a fisherman with a truth that guides him to the guarantee of catching speckled trout every time he can get his hook near those seagulls diving for those shrimp, for the speckled trout are right there in the water underneath those seagulls, and the speckled trout hit the fisherman's bait every time! NOW HERE'S A GREAT TRUTH that is the backbone of this book: A HUMAN BEING WITH THE TRUTH OF GOD CAN CAST ANYWHERE IN GOD'S CREATION AND CATCH THE LIFE OF CHRIST FOR THAT MOMENT, IMPACTING THEIR OWN LIFE OR THE LIFE OF SOMEONE ELSE ALL OF THE TIME. I see it happen every Sunday morning at a park on the south side of downtown Nacogdoches where I have been going for a little over three years now on Sunday mornings. "Christ In The Park." God's Truth "hooking" people and MAKING them free from the falsehoods of life. Well, amen.

Listen. Here is another great Truth: We are to SHARE any Truth God gives us. Actually, one of the greatest blessings in life is that we GET to share His Truth. It can bring great joy to our life to do so, and bring Christ's Life to those we take it to. An illustration of this is a memory I have of being down at the family beach shack one other time, and I met a fellow staying at the beach house across from our little place. It turns out he was a veteran of a foreign war, and was dealing with PTSD. After sharing with him for a good while the Truth of how God can heal emotions as well as bodies (and I believe God desires to heal any part of our soul as much as, if not more than, our body), God made this fellow free from some things he had been dealing with for quite a few years.

Did I mention "eyes" earlier? Oh, indeed. When my wife, Barbara, and I moved to Nacogdoches back in 2010, I went to see Dr. Robert Lehmann to get some new glasses. Dr. Lehmann is a noted specialist in cataract surgery. I was at the point where I was having difficulty reading with my glasses! Well, Dr. Lehmann said to me, "Lee, when you get tired of coming to me and getting a new prescription for new glasses, let me know. I can put some lenses into your eyes where you will not need any new glasses ever again." I was startled. New eyes? Never need new prescriptions? Well, long story short, he operated and put new lenses into my eyes. See??? I laughingly tell everyone I can now "see" the hairs inside a rabbit's nose @ 100 yards! And everything is brighter! The first time I walked into Wal-Mart after the surgery the brightness of their lights frightened me! Wow! "Once I was blind, now I can see!" That's what it is like when God opens our eyes and lets us "see" the TRUTH of His Word!

Not long after the surgery with Dr. Lehmann, I was down visiting Bruce once more, and as we were drifting an area I (yes, ME!) spotted some seagulls a long way off. "Bruce, seagulls! The birds are working over toward the eastern shoreline, past that point!" Bruce said, "I don't see any birds." WOW! My new eyes could see when Bruce's couldn't. He said, "Who is that doctor? I'm going to go get me some new eyes!" Two things: (1) we headed over and caught a limit under those birds. And, (2) I will tell you much more about Dr. Lehmann and "eyes" and "seeing" in chapter 15!

Before we move on, let me add something else about Bruce Baugh. Not only do I know he is a Born Again Believer, but Bruce is the epitome of my friend Michael Wells' analogy: "Truth is not only preached, it is demonstrated." Bruce's life is one that exemplifies the most uncomplicated, most humble, and most giving a Believer can live. Just as his Savior Jesus Christ lived those Truths, Jesus lives them through Bruce day in and day out. The Gospel writer John tells us that Jesus didn't live His life on His own. It was His Father living it through Him. And that Jesus now wants to Live His life through us. He Lives through the life we know as Bruce Baugh day after day.

Bruce and his wife, Carol, are enjoying Life to the fullest on the south side of Lake Charles, Louisiana, on the edge of Lake Calcasieu... or, Big Lake, as it is known to the locals. He is no longer a fireman... retired. He no longer chases thieves out into the parking lot of a Foley's/ Macy's as a part-time job. Retired. Today, Bruce is reaping all of the years of learning about trout and redfish. He is a full-time professional guide with a place set up to entertain and encompass a complete fishing experience. His calendar is filled Monday thru Friday during the peak seasons. It is a joy and a pleasure to stay in that large double-wide trailer for his fishing party of the next day. You come in, spend the night, get up way before daylight, head down to get ice and some breakfast and snacks, then go to wherever Bruce is launching for the day. Tideline Charters, Captain Bruce Baugh, 337-660-1814, www.tidelinecharterssllc.com. Get in touch with Bruce to see if the birds are working!

How does all this add up to a simple little book like this one? The Lord Jesus Christ IS Truth. He told us that in John 14:6,

> "I am the way, the truth, and the life. No man cometh
> unto the Father, but by Me"

God said in John 8:32,

> "And ye shall know the truth, and the truth shall make you
> free."

"Make" you free! I like that, don't you?!? Then God went further:

> "If the Son therefore shall make you free, ye shall be free
> indeed." (v.36)

Jesus IS Truth. Truth is everything. Truth is Freedom. Truth is Life. Truth is Peace. Truth is Love. Truth is Joy. Truth is a narrow, calm, uncomplicated path. Without Truth, life is hell here on earth, and for eternity also. In the next 16 chapters I am going to share great biblical Truths that different individuals have given to me. I will tell you how those Truths have impacted my life, and how they can impact yours. Every Truth in this book will work for you. And there are other Truths that are waiting out there in the waters of life you are about to ride through.

In one of the last chapters, I will share the stories of a few dear friends to whom God gave me the privilege of passing on some of these Truths, and let them tell you how they have impacted their lives. And in another of the last chapters, I will share a few other "mentors" with a brief recap of more great "Life Truths."

Each chapter can be read "on its own," a separate Truth that stands by itself to bring part of Christ's Life to our life. Let Captain Bruce Baugh and I take you on a fishing extravaganza to find where the seagulls are circling in your life…perhaps finding some of God's Truth that you need. So, grab your rod, tie on your favorite lure, and be ready to cast in any direction you like!

"Lord Jesus, Thank You for bringing Bruce Baugh into my life. The impact has been phenomenal that you have made through that moment of "The birds are working!" and ultimately the words, "Seagulls don't lie!," that rang a bell with all Your Truth. You are Truth. We want and need all of You we can get. Please give us all of Your Truth that You know we can handle, and make us free from any bondage we are in."

Oh, yes…I hope and pray God sends a Bruce Baugh into your life at just the right moment! And remember this…Truth will always find a way!

Chapter Two

John Morgan – "Ye Must Be Born Again"

"Marvel not that I said unto thee, ye must be born again."
John 3:7

Talk about divine appointments, the biggest one in the lives of Lee and Barbara McDowell took place on Sunday morning, May 18, 1980. Of course there had been many divine moments over the previous 30+ years leading up to this momentous encounter, but "THE moment" was around 10:00am that day in the gymnatorium of Sagemont Baptist Church (now called Sagemont Church) at 11323 Hughes Road in Houston, Texas. Barbara and I visited the church that Sunday morning "because our kids needed it."

John Morgan just celebrated his 52nd anniversary as Pastor of Sagemont Church in 2018. It was also the church's 52nd, as Pastor Morgan was the founding pastor. Sagemont is unquestionably one of the premier Baptist churches in America. And Pastor Morgan is also without question one of America's most renowned pastors. I often think of just how incredible, miraculous, almost unbelievable it is that Barbara and I visited Sagemont on THE Sunday that Pastor Morgan preached from the text, John 3:1-7, "Ye Must Be Born Again." John Morgan told us later it had been years since he had preached from that text. I can tell you that I don't think there could have been ANY OTHER message that would have so dramatically touched and reached our hearts as did the one that day.

Here is another astounding fact. Sometimes God can use the most hilarious reasons for man to act one way or the other, that most people wouldn't believe it to be the truth. But toward the end of the school year in 1980, our two girls were about to finish up another year at Frazier Elementary School on Hughes Road. Our oldest, Kelly, came home one day and told Barbara about some boy in her 4th grade class being kicked out of school for having wine in his lunchbox at school. Wow! A 4th grader having wine in his lunchbox at school. Now listen! God used that event to get our attention in a most unusual way. And reactions are oftentimes almost unpredictable. Here's a good example: we immediately thought that we must start attending church. The girls needed more than what we were able to give them at home. Do what??? How about that?!?

But with two very distinctively different church backgrounds, Barbara and I began to argue as to which church we would attend. We had just come off a somewhat disastrous participation at another local church a couple of years before (which was the first time we had been in church in years). So, we were both very careful to lay out our arguments as to why we should go to the one or the other. Then one Saturday morning, a guy named Dick Zimmerman, who was a Bus Captain with the Sagemont Baptist bus ministry, stopped by the house. It's what those bus captains and workers do every Saturday morning. They visit homes on their "route" over and over to remind the kids about some promotion on the bus the next day. However, Dick had spoken to Barbara several times in the past (I had been working Saturdays for years), and she had said she wouldn't let the girls ride the bus to SBC if we weren't going there. This Saturday I was in the yard working, having left the job I recently had. Dick stopped by, introduced himself, and once again asked if the girls could ride the bus the next morning. They were having a picnic after church, and their friend down the street wanted them to join her. As Dick and I discussed the fact that Barbara and I were once again talking about visiting a church but couldn't make up our mind, Dick gives us the most logical answer any bus captain could come up with on the spur of the moment: (remember now, a Baptist church had NEVER entered our discussion as to where we might start back to church! We had grown up in two very different churches from Baptist!). "Listen, why don't yall let the girls ride the bus, yall drive to SBC, and then next week you can decide which of those others you will visit the next week." Do what? Believe me, only a "lost" mind could take that and decide to go to the Baptist church!!!

Well, that's what happened. As we entered the door to SBC around 9:05 the next morning (we were 10 minutes early, didn't want to get there after the service had started and be noticed by everyone as we found a seat!), we sat down next to John and Mary Ella Elam. Of all people, John had sold us the house we lived in! After the singing and the welcoming of the visitors, the pastor, John Morgan, got up to preach. The Elams noticed we didn't have a bible with us. They had two. They loaned us one of theirs (novel idea for church members to be thinking!). The message was from the Gospel of John, chapter 3. I am not sure how we ended up on the right page, but we followed Bro. John (that's what Baptists used to call their pastor) as he read the first seven verses of chapter 3. There is no way I could explain it, but as he read verse 3...

> Jesus answered and said unto him (Nicodemus, the man in vs. 1 & 2), "Verily, verily I say unto thee, Except a man be born again, he cannot see the kingdom of God."

I have to tell you, I thought instantly: how can that happen??? And then Bro. John read verse 4...

> Nicodemus saith unto Him, "How can a man be born when he is old? Can he enter the second time into his mother's womb, and be born?"

Yes, Nicodemus...yes! HOW???

Bro. John read on: verses 5-7...

> Jesus answered, "Verily, verily, I say unto thee, Except a man be born of water and of the Spirit, he cannot enter into the kingdom of God. That which is born of the flesh is flesh; and that which is born of the Spirit is spirit. Marvel not that I said unto thee, Ye must be born again."

Wow! Somehow I grasped completely the difference between "except a man..." and "Ye must be..." Whew! What a difference. From a non-personal noun to a very personal pronoun. God's message hit home to me. I was grabbed by the TRUTH that I had to be Born Again.

The message ended, and what they call "an invitation" started. The music minister, Rick Weisinger, led the choir in an invitation song. Bro. John began asking folks to come and make a decision. I wanted to go, but with 1,000 people in that gym made into an auditorium that Sunday morning, and not knowing where those going forward were going, I held off. Besides, what would Barbara think or do?

Well, after church, the Elams guided us to the side of the stage where Bro. John was greeting visitors and giving each family a large Family Bible, a gift from the church to every visiting family every Sunday morning. (The church has continued giving the large Family Bibles to visitors to this day...38 years since we received ours! Now they give both English and Spanish translations). We met Bro. John (actually he knew us...he had come to visit us at our home in the years before), and he gave us the bible. We then were guided to a Sunday School room. And lo and behold, I run into Rick Jones, someone I had known from the work I used to do. We sat next to each other as Bill Sevier, the department director welcomed all, made a couple of announcements, and then called on Rick to lead us in prayer before we were to break up into 3 or 4 smaller groups for bible study (there were 30-40 people in that assembly room).

Let me tell you a truth that all church people ought to know: I was scared to death as Rick prayed. The thought that went through my mind was that if we came back next week Bill Sevier would ask me to pray in front of all those people...after all, I was sitting next to Rick, and Bill had heard that Rick and I knew each other...it was logical to my "lost" mind that I would be the one called on to pray next Sunday. I would not come back.

But, God intervened on the way home from church (while the girls had gone on the picnic with the bus kids, Mr. Zimmerman, and the other bus workers). About half-way in the 15 block ride back to our house, I turned to my wife, Barbara, and said: "I don't know about you, but according to what that preacher read in the Bible, and what all he said in the message, I am in trouble." Immediately, Barbara said she felt the same way. I said, "I will call in the morning and see if we can get an appointment to see the pastor to talk more about this."

Monday morning I called. My call was forwarded to Mrs. Beverly Chambers, Bro. John's assistant (she is still with him today!). The appointment was set for Tuesday morning around 10am at Bro. John's office at the church. Barbara and I went to the church Tuesday morning, May 20th, and during our visit with Bro. John he helped us to trust Jesus Christ as our very own personal Savior. Jesus is Lord. He is The Savior. He is OUR Savior.

It seems like almost instantly after we finished praying, Bro. John said: "You now have a NEW 'wanter'." New "wanter"? Bro. John continued, "Things you used to want, you will now not want. Things you used to not want, you will now want." Interesting. Then he turned to 2 Corinthians 5:17 and read:

> "Therefore if any man be in Christ, he is a new creature: old things are passed away; behold, all things are become new."

I like what Dr. W.A. Criswell says in his footnotes to this verse in his *The Criswell Study Bible*, "By the new birth the Christian has already undergone the fundamental change; he is a new creature of the sort that belongs in the new creation. A new creation, a new heaven and a new earth, is promised. (cf. Isaiah 65:17; Revelation 21:1)." Wow! I had no idea of all this when I was born again, but oh how it all is now TRUTH that God has revealed over the last 38 years! A new birth, a new family... that is the basis of Christianity. And God continues to reveal applications of the Truth of that verse.

2 Corinthians 5:17 is the first verse I ever memorized after becoming a Christian.

Interestingly, God had been up to several things in all this, one of which we were about to find out: Bro. John said, "I know someone we ought to call before you leave this morning." He picked up his office phone and called. "Bro. Dave, this is John Morgan. I have a couple in my office who just got Born Again, and I know you would want to know." After he gave the fellow our names, he handed the phone to me. On the other end was Dave Ragen, a former professional golfer I had known when I was playing on the PGA Tour. We spent time together in Florida one winter. Dave rejoiced at our trusting Christ, and we talked for several minutes. I must add that Dave and Geraldine had lived just down the street from us in Sagemont (right next door to the Seviers!), as he travelled the country with an evangelist who lived next door to us!

God is the God of "coincidences," isn't He! And, up to several things??? Dave used to call me every now and then, telling me he was in Tennessee, Florida, Georgia, wherever, and that he and the evangelistic team were praying for me to be Saved. Beautiful! (truth is: before May 20, 1980, after I got off the phone with Dave I would turn and say, "That fool calls me from wherever he is and tells me he is praying for me." Can't add the rest of what I would say!).

Here's one more: 2 weeks later, I started securing cassette tapes of the Sagemont services. As I listened to the one of the Sunday following our first visit (and salvation experience in Bro. John's office), Bro. John mentioned at the close of the service (it turned out to be a tape of the 2nd service that Sunday, and we had been in the first and came forward to publicly profess Christ), "A couple came forward in the first service that we (the church) have been praying for the past 6 years..." I about flipped out when hearing that! Imagine...the church praying for Barbara and me for six years!?!

The Truth will certainly make you free. Barbara and I have been "free" in Christ for over 38 years now. And all our family are Christians. Jesus Christ is The Way, The Truth, and The Life (John 14:6). We met The Truth, the Lord Jesus Christ, on that Tuesday morning of May 20, 1980, just before noon in Pastor John Morgan's office at Sagemont Baptist Church, Houston, Texas. And we have been free in the Lord ever since! Now for sure...there were not any seagulls flying around in the Sagemont worship service, or in Bro. John's office, BUT...there must have been some circling outside the building both of those days!

A little over 21 years later, Barbara and I flew to Seattle, Washington, to visit some friends who had been in the church I pastored in West Houston in the mid-90's. Brian and Jill Davis, and their two girls Allison and Sarah, made plans for us to do some sight-seeing. Jill found a beautiful cabin at the foot of Mt. Rainier for us to stay in for a few days. One of the first things we did was take a trip nearby to go see the volcano, Mt. St. Helens. What an incredible story and sight. What a blast! Now listen to this: for years I had told folks about Pastor Morgan's message from John, chapter 3, and say, "Just like a lead balloon falling on my head…wham! The truth crashed through." Well, at the Mt. St. Helens site, an amazing fact became known. Guess what?!? On May 18, 1980, at virtually the SAME TIME Pastor John Morgan was giving the invitation to trust in Christ in the church service at Sagemont Baptist Church in Houston, Texas, where we heard "Ye Must Be Born Again," MT. ST. HELENS ERUPTED. I've changed my story surrounding the impact of "Ye Must Be Born Again!"

The heart and soul of Christianity is the NEW BIRTH…a spiritual birth into a spiritual family.

Now listen. "Ye must be born again." All other Truths will be irrelevant if you have NOT been Born Again come judgment day. Included at the end of this book is a guide as to how you can Be Born Again… take the time to find it, ask someone about it, but do not fail to Be Born Again! There is so much to learn and appropriate in life concerning the two births: our physical birth and our need for the spiritual birth. Just as Jesus told Nicodemus in John ch. 3, they are two entirely and distinctively different births. The latter of which is a MUST to become a child of God. (In a future book I plan to delve into the many facets of the New Birth. Please search for all you can learn, ask God to give you His insights, and understand that with God there is nothing more important for you than that you become a Born Again Believer).

"Lord Jesus, my Savior, my All…I thank You for sending Pastor John Morgan and Sagemont Church into my life, and Barbara's, Kelly's, and Jennifer's lives, and working through everything in my life that was against You, and revealing Yourself to me and Barbara (and ultimately our whole family, including grandkids!) and drawing us to come to salvation through You in Pastor Morgan's office. I pray that ALL would come to this revelation and experience!"

Oh, yes…I hope and pray God sends a John Morgan into your life at just the right moment! And remember this…Truth will always find a way!

Chapter Three

Bill McDowell – "guilty by association"

"Come out from among them, and be ye separate, saith the Lord"
2 Corinthians 6:17

Here's an interesting remembrance: as the crow flies (much different than a seagull, lol!), when I was growing up in Baytown, Texas, we lived just a couple of miles from the salt waters of Trinity Bay, off Galveston Bay. I can remember the seagulls flying around near our home from time to time. Just an interesting bird to me back then, not knowing the significance that bird would play in my life some 25+ years later.

The 1950's and 1960's were a wonderful time to grow up in America. Although there were many homes where the Lord Jesus Christ was not the Savior of those in the families living therein, the Christian ethic was a domineering force. Very, very few kids grew up not knowing "right" from "wrong" according to Almighty God's teachings. And not only that, were held accountable for such. Tolerance was not a word of the day. "Kid's rights" were not thought of, much less talked about. And, it was a great day to be a kid.

Safety and innocence marked the lives of most kids. We wandered the streets on our bicycles…or, walked. We went places alone. And, our parents almost always knew exactly where we were, and where we had been. They had "eyes" all over town! And those "eyes" had mouths that didn't mind picking up the phone and giving a report to our parents! I remember several times my parents inquiring about my being somewhere different from where I told them I would be at a certain time. I remember several times my parents mentioning a call from a family friend that I "appeared" to be driving "a little too fast" down a neighborhood street.

But, let me be quick to tell you that I had two marvelous parents, a very loving and caring and supportive Dad, and a very loving and caring and supportive Mom. And I was fortunate to grow up in a home with two wonderful parents who were dedicated educators. And educators were among the most diligent to impress upon their kids the "rules." The lack of discipline was never an issue at my home! I remember my dad and mom telling me every time they gave me a whipping, "this is going to hurt me worse than it hurts you." It wasn't until I was a parent that I ever got an inkling of what that entailed.

I learned many life lessons from my parents. Things that even today at age 73, I still live by. I was loved by my parents, and I loved them. They both are in Heaven today.

My father, Bill McDowell, was a teacher, a coach, and a counselor. I had the privilege of learning math from him at a very early age. Since my elementary school was next door to the junior high where he taught, and we always got out of school earlier than the junior high did, I would go over and sit in on his last math class of the day. It was there I grew to have a love for math, and to become proficient at grade levels far beyond where I was in elementary school. Dad was also a coach. I had the privilege of being carried on the team bus way before I was old enough to be on the junior high teams. In fact, I can remember being carried IN the "ball bag" onto the bus, sitting on the steps just inside the door and looking out through the glass in the door as the road went by. I used to "keep the books" of Dad's basketball team when I was still in elementary school. Life lessons were innumerable.

Dad took me to several golf tournaments during the summers of my teen years. I was able to play in some state and national tournaments simply because he drove me to the tournaments at an age I didn't have a driver's license or car. On one in particular, we drove past the Augusta National Golf Club in Augusta, GA, on our way to Pinehurst, North Carolina. We thought we could just drive in, take a quick peek of the clubhouse...the 18th green...and then be on our way. Nope. They wouldn't let us in the gate. Well, trips like those lent themselves to some very interesting life lessons. Trip planning, money management, interaction with folks from different venues, etc., etc.

Another time, Dad and the father of another player (I won't mention his name for obvious reasons!) arranged for us to stay in a dorm room of a college while playing in the Texas State Jr. Championship. When we went out to eat, my friend's dad would say, "Jim (not his real name), you can have anything you want, but get _____ (the dad would name something). You can drink anything you want, but drink _____ (the dad would name something)." My father told me after that trip that he thought that was what he needed to start doing. Well, amen, he never did!

But, one lesson in particular he did teach me has carried with me these following 55+ years: "you can be guilty by association." What Dad taught me was this: no matter that you think different, act different, or have not participated in anything wrong…if you are "there" with the wrong-doers at the time the law (any authority) arrives, YOU are guilty also. He used to tell me over and over: "When the police show up, they will not go around and ask every one's name, and when they get to you, say, 'Oh, you are Bill McDowell's boy. I know you. I know your dad. I believe you when you say you were not doing what the others were doing… go on home.' They just won't do that."

Stop and think about it. What do you think when you come up on something that is "not right," and you see who all is present. How often do you wonder if there is any who were NOT participating in the "wrong" action? You, see?

To my Dad and Mom (Mildred Elizabeth "Beth" McDowell) it was very important with whom I was running around. They were always attuned to who my friends were. They were constantly asking questions, wanting to meet the parents of my friends. Actually, since my mother was a teacher also…3rd grade…she and Dad knew through school contacts and events the parents of most every friend I ever had. And they had teacher friends who could fill in the blanks for them!

What is God trying to tell us about with "whom" we associate, and why? Well, let us look at two or three more scripture references: 1 Corinthians 13:6 – "(Love) rejoiceth not in iniquity, but rejoiceth in the truth."

Psalm 97:10 – "Ye that love the LORD, hate evil…"
Psalm 37:27, 32 – "Depart from evil, and do good…
The wicked watcheth the righteous and seeketh to slay him."

Unequivocally, God doesn't want us to "associate" with evil, iniquity, anything that is wrong, not those who are doing such. This is a real lesson to learn: beware, we can associate with the wrong people, the wrong activities, and be "guilty by association."

One way my Dad also influenced whom I was associated with was he would take me and some friends on camping trips. McCollum Park, a small Chambers County park off Tri-City Beach Road east of Baytown was a favorite spot for Dad, me, and four or five other guys (and sometimes the father of one of the boys). McCollum Park was named for the father of a friend of mine in the 4th and 5th grades…H.H. McCollum, Chambers County Commissioner, was the father of Randy McCollum, my friend. We slept in tents with sleeping bags. We cooked on an open fire. We crabbed off the long pier in the waters of Trinity Bay. We hiked the countryside near the park. We explored the banks of the bay for driftwood and debris hunting for "treasures." We sat around the fire at night talking about "life." McCollum Park is where I learned to snipe hunt. Ask any man born in the 40's or 50's if they have ever been "snipe hunting."

I hope there are some dads or granddads who are reading this that will take heed to the beauty of being involved in their kid's lives. Much of what I had the privilege to participate in as a kid is non-existent in many kids' lives today. Our friends, Gary & Anne Marie Ezzo (Growing Families.Life) always have said, "More is caught than taught." One of the greatest ways for parents to teach, lead, and insure their kids are learning a lesson that can keep them innocent in the growing up years, AND in the adult years, is to teach that whom we associate with speaks volumes to a watching world. "Guilty by association" can be a POSITIVE as well as a NEGATIVE.

Now, listen, my dad did not teach me most of these things from a deep scriptural perspective, at least not quoting Scripture while he taught. We went to the church right down the street from our home, but the Bible was not that dominant in our home (or that church!). Christianity was the steering world view, but certain scriptures were not taught or memorized. It was only after getting into church at age 35, and being Born Again, that God's Word began to become alive in regard to some of the teachings I had been given at an earlier age.

God tells us in His Word things like:

"Be ye not unequally yoked together with unbelievers:
for what fellowship hath righteousness with
unrighteousness? and what communion hath light with
darkness?" 2 Corinthians 6:14
"Wherefore come out from among them (those
mentioned in the previous verse), and be ye separate, saith
the Lord, and touch not the unclean thing…"
2 Corinthians 6:17
"Abstain from all appearance of evil." 1 Thessalonians 5:21

Back in my grade school and teen years there were places I was not to go. There were things my parents taught me not to do. There were people I was instructed not to associate with. And today, as an older adult (with Holy Spirit indwelling me, and Him as my Shepherd), there are places I could go, but I don't. There are things I could do, but I don't. There are folks I could associate with, but choose not to. My parents are not here to watch me, control me, even discipline me. But, I don't do some things, or go some places, that I could. God is with me ALL the time. He is very capable of disciplining me. But, I am always cognizant that He never takes away the choices I can make.

I had the joy and privilege to do something as a 17-yr. old kid that many would never do today. I flew alone to Detroit, Michigan, to play in the 1962 USGA National Jr. Boys Golf Championship. After that tournament, I travelled alone by train to Minneapolis, Minnesota, for the Western Golf Assoc. Jr. Boys Championship. What a trip! What an experience! And the train trip took me through Chicago, Illinois, where I had to change train stations! Carrying a golf bag and two suitcases, I had to go way across town…taking a taxi to get from the South Side of Chicago to the North Side. Wow! Life is different today! So much of the early life lessons my parents had taught me took me through some of the most incredible experiences a young 17-yr. old could imagine. I made many choices on that trip whether to be involved with different people, or not. Truth guards the heart.

So, why do I choose to not associate with some people? Why do I choose to not do some things? Why do I choose to not go some places? There is one thing that I have shared several times (from the pulpits I was privileged to speak from) that was prevalent in my mind as a teenage boy growing up in Baytown, going to Horace Mann Junior High School, then Robert E. Lee High School. There were many instances where I was faced with temptations to participate in something that I knew I shouldn't be doing, and the ONE thing that came to my mind over and over was this: "If I were to get caught, it would embarrass and hurt my Dad and Mom a whole lot more than it would me." And I didn't want that to occur.

Here's a question for you: has it ever crossed your mind that if you got caught, or someone who might know you (or, perhaps may ever someday know you!) saw what you were doing…have you ever thought of whether your actions would bring any hurt or embarrassment to the Lord Jesus Christ? Or, your associating with certain people may do the same? Well, would you want that to happen?

Let me share 7 guidelines that are always on my mind:

1. It is always right to do what is right.

2. It is never right to do what is wrong.

3. Hanging with, or associating with, those doing wrong is not right.

4. I don't want to harm my reputation.

5. I don't want to harm God's reputation.

6. And even though my parents (and grandparents) are dead and gone, I don't want to harm their reputation. There are still many people alive today who knew my parents and grandparents.

7. And...there are others (some of whom are part of this book's focus) of whom I would not want to in any way harm their reputation by any actions of mine.

I thank God, and I praise God, for my parents He gave me 73 years ago on June 1, 1945, in Commerce, Texas, at Allen Hospital. I thank God, and I praise God, for my grandparents God also gave me...O. B. (Brad) & Mildred (Mil) Bradford and Maurine (WaWa) McDowell. I thank God, and I praise God, for my wife – Barbara; our oldest daughter – Kelly, her husband – Chad, the two grandkids they have blessed us with - Darby & Garrett; our youngest daughter – Jennifer, her husband – Braxton, and the two grandkids they have blessed us with – Braden & Ashleigh. I add Barbara and the other family members at the top of the list of those I do not want to in any way harm their reputation by any actions of mine.

Coming out from, and being separate from, are more than just a few words from God. They are a lifestyle that is protective, productive, and preventative of many things that provide the vehicle that God Himself can Live through with no hindrances. This Truth has guided me to where God wanted me to be more times than I can count and protected me in just as many ways. To that I say, "Amen!"

"Lord Jesus, Thank You for my father, Bill McDowell. Thank You for giving me the perfect father for my life. I know my life choices are always up to me. You have given clear instruction on a lot of what, where, and who...even why we choose certain ones and certain things to be a part of our life, and stay away from others. Thank You, that You are always present with me as I make choices...Shepherding me to make Your choice. I trust You."

Oh, yes...I hope and pray God has given you a father like Bill McDowell, even if it is a moment later in life (soak on that idea) and is just the right moment! And remember this...Truth will always find a way!

Chapter Four

O.B. Bradford – "Keep your hook in the water!"

"But ye shall receive power, after that the Holy Ghost is come upon
you: and Ye shall be witnesses unto me both in Jerusalem, and in all
Judea, and in Samaria, and unto the uttermost part of the earth."
Acts 1:8

Acts 1:8 is one of the most dramatic moments in biblical history.
Jesus is giving His last words spoken on this earth just before He
ascended to Heaven…my, oh my, what a historic moment also.

And profound.

Jesus speaks 39 words, covering Holy Ghost power, witnessing, and
really the whole of the discovered and known Earth at that time. What in
the world (no pun intended!) did His closest disciples think when He said
this to them? He is instructing them to be His witnesses with all power
(Holy Spirit with them, in them, and through them) in all places. And they
were about to begin sharing the Gospel of the Lord Jesus Christ "world-
wide." Yes, they would do things to "earn a living," or to "provide for
them and their family," but they were IN His ministry. The rest of the
New Testament is a guide for today's Believers as to many ways to "do"
this ministry. Wow!

I remember my start into fishing. My grandfather, O. B. Bradford, of
Commerce, Texas (my mother's father), started taking me fishing when I
was two years old. I have been "hooked" on fishing ever since!

It wasn't with a scripture in mind, but the most profound truth my
grandfather taught me about fishing was this: "Son, I have never caught
a fish in the air, in a tree, or in the boat…keep your hook in the water!"
With that, my grandfather gave me a wonderful example that has
transcended into one of life's greatest lessons with a total scriptural
context. I was a young boy at the time Brad (that's what everyone called
my grandfather, including me and other family members) spoke those
words to me while we were fishing out of one of his own homemade,
flat-bottom, wood boats…custom-designed to fish in small farm ponds
or fishing lakes (free diagrams for anyone interested).

And, over 30 years later, one day in my initial time of serving as the Outreach Leader for Bill Sevier's YA1L Sunday School department at Sagemont Church, the thought crossed my mind: just as my grandfather gave me that truth about catching fish, God spoke to my heart this same premise about "catching souls."

(YA1L was short for "Young Adult One Late"…1st age grouping for Young Adults, "late" Sunday School…church @ 9:15, SS @ 10:45…more about Bill Sevier in chapter 13)

Shucks, in my years of selling cars and boats, I had practiced my grandfather's advice by trying to stay in front of a prospective customer, dangling the sales pad in front of them consistently while "asking for the order" in the closing office, etc. ("catching a customer")…you know how a good salesman is persistent.

I remember sitting in my grandfather's lap as a 2 yr-old, on the banks of the Roundhouse Pool at the Commerce, Texas, train depot. The trains didn't run through Commerce. It was like a dead-end. There was this huge revolving mechanism that would "turn" the engines around, and once the cars were hooked back up, the trains would head out of town back toward Greenville the same way they came in. That's where the Roundhouse got its name. The pool, as I remember it, was for water needed for train engines. The pool also held many, many small perch, or bream, as we called them. Brad tried to help me catch ALL the bream out of that pond! It truly is as the old saying goes…I was "hooked."

I even remember one day later as a 7-8 yr. old catching 144 bream with Brad on a small fishing lake he was a member of outside Honey Grove, a town north of Commerce. It was sweet catching all those fish that day! Get this: we didn't have a "stringer" or a "fish basket"…or a "live well." Brad made a "fish bag" out of a feed towsack. He strung a cord through one end he opened, and he would tie the towsack onto the boat (he had constructed a special board running the entire length on the inside of the gunwale of his homemade boats just for tying off anchors or the fish bag!). He opened it when he put another fish into the sack. Almost a full towsack that day! Oh, yes, we had to go through Bug Tussle on state highway 34, at the intersection of FM 1550, 8.3 miles south of Honey Grove. I have to tell you, these are very sweet memories for an old fishing boy like me! I still have a picture in my mind of the shape of that small lake, the large cattails and lily pads, the place where several private boats were pulled up on the bank and locked to a tree with a chain and padlock, AND I even picture one particular spot where Brad caught a small bass while we were fishing for bream. But there was this particular set of lily-pads where we must have caught 25 nice bream. Brad called that a "bream bed."

I still have a couple of the turkey quills Brad used to make what he called a special bream cork, lightweight enough and slender enough for us fishermen to see a sensitive touch of the bream on that worm on the hook! It seemed to wiggle ever so slightly when a bream would first breathe on the bait! We would adjust the quill so that there was about two feet of line between the hook and the quill. We would "slip" our line out, the hook and worm with a small weight would start toward the bottom, and then the quill would stand straight up. Well, the fish were biting so fast and furious that the quill never had time to "stand up"! Just about the time the quill would begin to go erect, the bream grabbed the worm and took off…the quill darting under the water and disappearing. Have you ever caught a nice-sized bream on a cane pole, or a fly rod?!? To a 7-8 yr. old boy it is like catching a 5-lb bass (or, 7-lb speckled trout) on a rod and reel! Hang on!

From the Roundhouse pool to catching fish in Doc Allen's farm pond, to the Club Lake outside the small town of Honey Grove, to Lake Lydia (a private lake with many cabins around it, one of which my grandparents owned), to the early days of the flooding and filling of Lake-O-the-Pines (all these are East Texas fishing spots), to a ditch running alongside the Highlands Reservoir outside Baytown, Texas…each fishing trip with Brad hinged on one thing: how long were our hooks in the water. Grandpa always "out-fished" me when it came to having his hook in the water more than I did!

By the way, Bruce Baugh is as persistent about having his hook in the water as my grandfather was! Cast, twitch. twitch, twitch, twitch… reel, cast, twitch, twitch…

I tried counting one day, and got tired keeping track. But I figured Bruce had his bait in the water approximately 40% more time than I did!

I have some absolutely wonderful memories of my grandfather and me "wetting a hook" in different places. That's a truth that shouldn't escape any of you grandfathers. After Brad had graduated from Texas A&M with an Agricultural degree, he was with East Texas State Teachers College (now Texas A&M University/Commerce) for 50 years - first as an Agriculture teacher, then as Head of the Ag Dept., then heading up all the maintenance at the college before he retired. I remember his house on Campbell Street in Commerce that had two bait sources: one was a small evergreen bush at the front porch, always possessing some "bag worms." Bag worms (as Brad called them) were a small worm less than an inch long but rather "fat," housed in a brown bag made from the bush's "leaves." Brad would send me out with a small paper sack to gather 25 or so off the bush. It was fun for this small boy to get my quota, twist the top on the sack, then listen as the worms eased out of their "bag" and started scratching their way trying to find a way out of the paper bag. I can still hear the sound of those worms! And the best thing about bag worms…they were a cinch to catch a bream or goggle-eye! The fish couldn't resist them (sort of like water dogs and bass!). Also, always available, a second source was Brad's worm bed. Earthworms, he called them. Three to four inches long, skinny, wriggling dudes! And the worm bed was a #2 metal washtub about half-filled with special ingredients. Best I remember, coffee grounds were a staple. Left-overs of celery, lettuce, tomatoes, etc. from a salad bowl from lunch or supper were good. Good soil was also something used. Interesting thing about the worm bed in the metal washtubs: the tub must be kept in a relatively cool place. Where better than under the house? Yes, the house, like many in that day, was not built on a concrete slab but on concrete blocks…about 18 inches off the ground. Perfect for putting a #2 washtub under! A moist feedsack covering the "bed" in the washtub was great for keeping it cooler and not allowing it to dry out. Earthworms like a "moist" soil.

Now, listen, The Word of God is God's perfect bait for fishing for men. Romans 10:17 tells us:

> "So then faith cometh by hearing, and hearing by the word of God."

I will always tell everyone that if you want to see God catch a lost soul, share the Word of God with that lost soul. Man's words, man's ways and methods, and man's ideas are no substitute for the Word of God!

When I was about 10 years old, one summer I was spending a few weeks at my grandparent's home in Commerce. After lunch I would lay in bed in front of the window that had a gadget that my grandfather had designed and built (one for almost all the windows in the house) that was like a "cage" filled with a "hay-like" material. It had a copper tube crossing the top that had several tiny holes where water passing through the tube would drip down on the material. A big attic fan in the house hallway drew a breeze from the outside in through the wetted material, turning the air into a cool "air-conditioned" room. I would lay there listening to the baseball game on the radio (no TV at that time!). The biggest thrill, other than the NY Yankees (with Mickey Mantle, my hero) winning a game, was to get a call from Brad telling me to gather some worms, and we would head out to Dr. Allen's farm pond after he got off work. On Saturdays is when we would get the truck loaded and drive to that Club Lake he belonged to outside the small town of Honey Grove. I have to repeat myself: I can still picture the day we loaded a feed sack with 144 bream!

I can still picture us many times scaling, cleaning, and putting fish into all kinds of pans filled with water to freeze them to save for later eating. My grandfather had a one car garage, separate from the house, with a dirt floor. He built a covered area onto the back of the garage (lean-to roof). Under that cover, he built a cooking counter, complete with a cast-iron kettle with some sort of gas cooker underneath. Frying fish and hush-puppies (Brad's homemade recipe) was a real event for this young boy! My grandmother, Mil (short for Mildred), was in the kitchen making coleslaw and some sort of special dessert (Brad's favorite was peach cobbler).

Can you believe that as I sit here writing (around 60+ years later) I can picture in my mind those fabulous fishing trips with my grandfather? How about me seeing in my mind, from 38 years ago, the first person I saw pray to trust Christ as their Savior (I see his kitchen table right now!) who had visited our church, come to our Sunday School class, heard Pastor John Morgan preach several messages, his wife come to trust Christ as her personal Savior...several times the "bait" was cast out to him... and then that Saturday morning in his kitchen he was ready to "bite."

Wow! A perfect spiritual example of "keeping our hook in the water."

Now here's a point and a question I have: every fisherman dreams of the day that virtually every time he casts his bait into the water, a fish bites. Every Christian would love to have someone positively respond every time they invite the person to church, or to a relationship with Christ. ARE people "biting" the Christian "bait" like they used to back in the mid-1900's?

OR, have you noticed how few Christians are "fishing" for Lost Souls these days? For the last 25 years I have noticed that there are hardly any church members (who are supposed to be Christians) who go out "fishing for souls." Church visitation has become a thing of past years. Even passing out "bait" (flyers or other pieces of info about church or Christ...you know, the Christian's bag worms or earth worms!) has become virtually non-existent. This is really incredible, isn't it? JESUS SAID, "**Ye shall receive** power, after that the Holy Ghost is come upon you: and **Ye shall be** witnesses unto Me both in Jerusalem, and in all Judea, and in Samaria, and unto the uttermost part of the earth" (Acts

1:8). HE ALSO SAID, "**Go ye therefore**, and teach all nations, baptizing them in the name of the Father, and of the Son, and of the Holy Ghost: **Teaching them** to **observe** all things whatsoever I have commanded you: **and, lo, I am with you always,** even unto the end of the world. Amen." (Matthew 28:19-20). (my emphasis with bold print)

I understand many folks use the "lifestyle evangelism" approach to witness to their family, friends, and neighbors. But, let me add that it has been my experience to note that the devil, who is the father of all lies, deceit, and counterfeiting is an expert in taking one small "deficiency" in every Christian's character and making an excuse for an Unbeliever to stay away from church. I know that it was an incident in a Christian neighbor's life that once kept us out of church. In fact, it was 5 years later before we ever went to any church, and a couple of years after that before we went to Sagemont Baptist (and remember, that was because "the kids needed it").

That is why we must be keeping our "hook" with some "good bait" in front of the unchurched and Unbelievers constantly. The Apostle Paul showed us as an example. And his persistent "fishing" yielded lots of "catches." Even though every once in a while the "fish" just weren't biting…"almost thou persuadeth me to be a Christian," said King Agrippa to Paul (Acts chapter 26). Well, amen.

Listen…my grandfather, O. B. Bradford, NEVER told me I could or would catch any fish by the way I dressed, the way I talked, how new or how fancy my rods and reels were, how big or well-equipped the boat was that we went fishing in…you get the idea! Well, I must admit, he did have one odd piece of advice: "Son, if you're not catching anything, try spitting on the worm next time before you toss it into the water." Now, I don't advise that idea when witnessing to Unbelievers! No, sir, just stick to Brad's famous words: "keep your hook in the water!"

By the way, when you learn how to "put the bait on the hook correctly"…using the best ways to design and produce the materials you are using for "bait" to attract new members, the results are always best.

Let me give you one more magnificent truth: A REAL fisherman can't stand the thought of laying down his rod and not making one more cast, and having to head for home, unless he has had a "good catch" for the day. The same is truth for a soul fisherman. John Morgan once told me that when they first started Sagemont Church he would ask God to give him at least one new member each week, and he started out on Mondays going knocking on doors in the neighborhood, casting the "hook" to try and find new members – not stopping before the next

Sunday until God had given him a "catch." That's "keeping your hook in the water"!!!

Now, listen, whether you are trying to "catch a new soul," find a new church member, sell whatever product, OR find a new friend...the same truth applies: KEEP YOUR HOOK IN THE WATER!

Wait a minute...one more significant Truth my grandfather gave me: "No one can make decisions for you, no one will look out for you, except yourself. Be a decision-maker." Personal responsibility. Let me make one final point: You must make the decision to be a "witness" or "soul winner." Will you?

> "The fruit of the righteous is a tree of life; and he that
> winneth souls is wise." Proverbs 11:30

I certainly don't recall any real seagulls circling that private lake in North Texas, or the Roundhouse Pond, or Doc Allen's pond, back when I was a young boy learning to "keep my hook in the water." But, over the years, there have been hundreds of times when "the hook in the water" caught something! It is Truth that has MADE a difference.

"Lord Jesus, I thank You that you gave me O. B. Bradford to be my grandfather. The 'catch' is always up to You. You simply have told us You wanted to make us fishers of men. Keep reminding us of our necessity to be prepared AND to be persistent in keeping our baited hook in the water of souls surrounding us."

Oh, yes...I hope and pray God has given you a grandfather like O. B. Bradford. And remember this...Truth will always find a way!

Chapter Five

W. D. (Bill) Hinson – "Son, you've bought it…"

"A good name is rather to be chosen than great riches,
and loving favor rather than silver and gold."
Proverbs 22:1

My oldest memory of William Dennis ("Bill") Hinson is as a very young boy. Each Christmas I would get this phone call with a hearty "ho-ho-ho-ho" coming over the phone line, and I knew Santa Claus was calling and wanting to know what I was desiring for Christmas. Mr. Hinson's deep voice was scintillating to this kid whom the first time was barely old enough to talk on a phone. Over the years I grew to respect every word that came out of his mouth.

Mr. Hinson (as we still called him up to his graduation to heaven at age 98+) was the oldest friend (# of years, and age) I recall our family knowing. He graduated from Winnsboro High School around 1925, and at the age of 16 went to East Texas State Teachers College in Commerce. My grandfather, O.B. Bradford, and grandmother, Mildred, had a garage apartment they rented out to college students. My grandfather (we called him Brad) taught at the college at that time. Brad had graduated from Texas A&M around 1920, and taught agriculture at ETSTC.

My mother, Mildred Elizabeth Bradford McDowell (everyone called her Beth) loved to tell stories of how she was a small toddler when Mr. Hinson came to stay in their garage apartment at the house on Bonham street. She said Mr. Hinson didn't mind her chewing on his ankles… LOL!...as she crawled around the house and found him sitting at the kitchen table or in the living room.

From those early years in my life, the Hinsons have been a part of my family even to this day with the Hinson's daughter, Mary DelHomme, still a dear, dear friend. I could tell jillions of funny, serious, delightful, enlightening stories of memories that God gave me (and my wife, Barbara, and our two girls, Kelly & Jennifer) over the years. But, one in particular fits the bill to be in this "hall of honor" book:

51

Mr. Hinson tells of the time he and Mrs. Hinson (her name was Lillian, but somehow as a young kid I called her Ennie) went back home to East Texas from Weinert, TX, a "one-block town" as the Hinson's daughter, Mary, recalls her parents talking about it. This is where they had gotten their first jobs out of college. Mr. Hinson and his father went to town. One of their stops was at the local gas station/grocery/car dealership. And the proprietor got to talking with Mr. Hinson about trading up to a new car now that he had a steady job. Mr. Hinson would say, "new always smells much better than what you currently have!"

So the "bug" kind of bit him, and before long the two men had come to an agreement on a "good price" for a trade. Mr. Hinson's father had finished his shopping and had gassed up, and the two Hinson men headed back home. Along the way, a huge LIFE CHANGING moment occurred for Mr. Hinson. He said to his father, "I don't think I should go through with that trade." (Remember, he hadn't even said one word to Ennie. I don't know why we didn't call her Mrs. Hinson!). As soon as the words came out of Mr. Bill Hinson's mouth…he tells the story such… his father exclaimed, "Son, you have done bought that car! You gave the man YOUR WORD that you agreed with the price and agreed to get the new car. Son, You HAVE bought it."

Do you understand what happened? Back in that day and time, a man's WORD meant everything. When a man SAID something, it was a "done deal," as they used to say. Mr. Hinson had SAID he would trade. Mr. Hinson had SAID he agreed to the price differential. Mr. Hinson's NAME was at stake, according to his father. And, in that day and time, his father's NAME was at stake! It's sort of funny, but I don't ever recall hearing what Ennie said to Mr. Hinson when she found out about him making this trade without even mentioning anything to her beforehand. Guess it slipped my mind to inquire about that…

But, now listen, what a difference several years can make. In THIS day and time, a MAN'S WORD (for most men) isn't worth the time, effort, and air used to make the proclamation. How sad so many men have sunk to such a low level of character! NEVER MR. HINSON.

Do you get the connection between this moment in Mr. Hinson's life and his word in relation to God's Word of Proverbs 22:1? WOW! The wisest man to ever live, King Solomon, proclaimed to us that a man's word, his name tied to his word, is rather to be chosen than great riches. Do you get the connection of where men, boys, women, and girls are today with our "words." My goodness, how low have we sunk? How degraded have our thoughts and words become? Corruption, depravity, debased, degenerate…how sad the difference of character from a "man of his word" to the lowest of low in life.

I have always praised God that the course of my life involved my family being a part of the W. D. Hinson family and their lives. The wisdom, the guidance, the character that was imparted my way has had a dramatic impact on choices I have made, directions I have headed, and a constant reminder of how important and critical is each and every word that comes out of my mouth.

A few years after that car trade incident, Mr. Hinson went to Baytown, Texas, to go to work for the Goose Creek Consolidated Independent School District. As you might imagine, a bright future awaited this wonderful couple. Mr. Hinson became the Principal of Horace Mann Jr. High School. And in 1950, after my parents had lived in Robstown, Texas (home of the Robstown Cottonpickers!...the school's mascot), for a couple of years at their first job of teaching out of college, Mr. Hinson hired my dad to come to Horace Mann to teach and coach. I was 5 years old. The years of family connection and gatherings continued.

The first home I remember the Hinsons living in was on the west side of Baytown. Bayshore Drive, I believe. They had what my sister considered a "fancy" home. It was located on what was a small peninsula extending out into one of the smaller bodies of water near the Houston Ship Channel. I remember several things about that home. It was BIG (especially to this young boy). It was WHITE (Mrs. Hinson loved white carpet, white furniture, her white piano! It was even that white stone/brick on the outside). They had many azalea bushes all around the house and in the yard, AND…it had a back yard that sloped down to the water. I didn't know it at the time, but the seagulls flying around would come to play a significant role in my life.

Sometime around my 7th or 8th birthday, my grandparents and the Hinsons both purchased small cabins on a small lake called Lake Lydia, just east of Quitman, Texas. What a grand place for a young boy to fish and explore the "wilds." Mr. Hinson and Brad used to love to "kid" each other and play jokes on each other. One time we were at the lake the day before the Hinsons were coming. I think it might have been a Thanksgiving or some holiday. Anyway, my grandfather got this wild idea: he, my dad, and I took some Catfish Charlie (stink bait for baiting a trotline for catfish) and put balls of it on the springs of the bed in the Hinson's cabin. Hooooooo-boy! What an odor when the Hinsons arrived! What is so funny is that Mr. Hinson and Brad stood out in the yard laughing so hard while Ennie was virtually in tears at what to do with the smell. A good man, with a good name, doesn't mind having a good time, even at his own expense!

I remember when I graduated from Horace Mann, the end of my 9th grade in 1960. (High School didn't start until the 10th grade back then). The Hinsons gave me my first "savings account." They opened the account at a bank there in Baytown, and started me on the wise course of not spending every dollar I made but putting at least "something" away for a later need. (that will be a chapter in a book I am compiling on the connection between "math" and "life").

There was the time not long after when I came home from some school event to find the Hinsons at my home on South Circle Drive. My grandmother, Mil, had passed away, and they were there to comfort my parents and my sister and me. I can picture that moment in my mind today as I sit and type about it. In the weeks to follow, my sister, Lynn, and I would spend some weekends with the Hinsons while my Dad and Mom went to Commerce to be with my grandfather.

Again and again, our paths would cross. And year after year, the stories would flow from Mr. Hinson's lips telling of life as a Christian, as an educator, as a man whose word meant more than anything else to him.

Let me ask you this: how many times have you told someone you would do something, be somewhere, buy this or that…spoken a "word"… that you knew you had to follow through with, OR your NAME would be "tarnished"? Does THAT ever cross your mind? Have you ever even stopped to think of that happening? Does your NAME mean anything to you, or what someone else thinks when they think of or hear your NAME? This is a Truth that will be worth more than anything the world has to offer you!

Years later, I don't recall actually seeing or hearing any seagulls diving into any water at any time I was at the Hinson's when they lived on the north side of Houston (where Mr. Hinson told me the story of the "new car"), but Truth was always present just the same. Jesus was always there. Anytime I was near the Hinsons.

"Lord Jesus, Thank You for giving me and my family such a wonderful family friend as W. D. (Bill) Hinson in our lives. He and his wife, Lillian (Ennie), were truly a gift from You. You have spoken to me just how much that a 'Good Name' is important to You, and should be to me. Lord, may You always walk with me and help me to watch over the name You have given me."

Oh, yes…I pray God sends a W. D. "Bill" Hinson into your life at just the right moment! And remember this…Truth will always find a way!

Chapter Six

Bill Shelton – "This is the closest place to the clubhouse"

"I have fought a good fight, I have finished my course,
I have kept the faith."
2 Timothy 4:7

It is easy to quit something. Just give up. Perhaps blame others for our misfortune. Oftentimes that decision is made without the person even thinking about it, or that it has been made. But some place deep inside a person, there is a part that decides to quit or to keep-on-keepingon. That's why I have often attributed my sports background to giving me my first opportunities (and 1,000's since!) to face making those decisions. With a dad who was a coach, and being involved in sports since I was four or five years old (I remember being put into the ball bag when my dad was coaching basketball, carried onto the bus, then scrambling out to sit on the steps of the bus just inside the doors, looking out onto the road and roadside as the team travelled to an "away" game), I learned what it meant to face life's challenges and never quit. But there was one moment in my life that has definitely defined the last 58 years...

I met William F. (Bill) Shelton when I had just turned 12 years old (June, 1957). It was "happenstance" to some, but later I came to know it was part of God leading me on the path He had for my life. When I say "happenstance," it is because I had what some would say was an "unfortunate accident" while playing Little League baseball. One night I was pitching for the Humble Pelicans in the South League of Baytown Little League baseball. In the bottom half of one inning as I was standing in the batter's box waiting to hit next, another kid came by swinging a bat (he was supposed to be in the dugout!). His bat struck my right elbow, and it hurt like the dickens. Just a couple of innings later, as I tried to continue pitching, my arm stiffened completely to the point I couldn't continue to play. My dad took me to the doctor who gave me a cortisone shot (I remember the doctor strapping me down so I couldn't move AND see the needle that seemed 6" long!), and said to me: "You will have to give up most sports, because if it gets hurt again you could end up with a stiff arm for the rest of your life." That hurt worse than the elbow!!!

Up to that time, I had never hit a golf ball except for maybe a swing or two while out caddying for my dad at the old Humble Club next to the ship docks in the Humble Oil & Refining Company refinery in west Baytown. I think Dad and the coaches he would play with liked me watching carefully for their drives, because the cracks in the "black gumbo" in the hot summertime were so wide a ball could get as far down into the ground as a foot or so, even in the fairway! "Black gumbo" (hard black soil baked by the scalding summertime sun) is something everyone in southern Texas learns to deal with. Well, if the flight of the ball wasn't "marked" carefully, there might be no way to know just where the ball could be. Anyhow, after the doctor released me to be active again, my dad took me to the Atascocita Country Club golf course beside Lake Houston, near the town of Humble, Texas. Bill Shelton was the Head Pro at the golf course. Leonard Jacobson was his assistant. Atascocita was the poor man's country club. A rich man owned the place, and he made it affordable for working people to belong and play. People drove for miles and miles to play there. It was new. I remember the annual membership fee was like $6, and green fees were $1.00 on weekdays, $1.50 on weekends. Bill was a young pro in his first Head Pro club job. As my dad told the story of my injury, and that I was considering taking up the game of golf, Bill suggested we take some used clubs out to the driving range and see what might fit me. He said used clubs would be the best thing to start with since we didn't know if I would even stick with playing. Keep this in mind. Those used clubs were made by the Spalding company.

An incredible moment of my life happened within 10 swings of the club I was first using. Bill Shelton turned to my dad and me and said, "All club pros like to have a young boy whom they call *their boy*." He continued, "When the pros gather at a tournament or meeting, they love bragging that *my boy* beat *your boy!*" Mr. Shelton was speaking of the tournament competition offered by the great junior golf program operated by the Houston Golf Association each summer. Bill Shelton then made a proposition that changed my life. He said he would start giving me lessons (if I promised to not take lessons from anyone else), give me a job at the course on weekends to start earning some money to pay for golf tournaments, and help me to become a competitive player. Golf right there and then replaced most other sports in my life.

I could fill a whole book on the stories about my golfing days at the Atascocita Country Club back in the late 50's and early 60's. I can remember so many people I was fortunate to meet and play with on that course. I remember Wayne Robbins, owner of Robbins Chevrolet, and his brother, Sonny, an attorney in Humble. I remember Joe Mack Walker, owner of a TV store in Humble. I remember playing with Boots and Coots Matthews of Red Adair's fire-fighting team. Bud McFaddin, former pro football player. Bill's daughter, Debbie Shelton, and Cynthia Marsh, were two of my playing buddies, and really good! I also remember getting beat by a guy named Jimmy in the club championship one year. On the 1st extra hole of match play. I wasn't very "sportsmanlike" walking off that green! I can remember caddying for Homero Blancas, who was a star on the Univ. of Houston golf team, while he was competing in a tournament the Univ. of Houston was hosting at Atascocita (Homero hit 18 greens in regulation that day, 2-putted every one, shooting even par 72). Leonard and Catherine Jacobson were such a big help to me and my family. In the early days of working at the course on weekends, my dad drove me to the course before daylight on Saturday mornings and then returned that evening to get me. Then he drove me back Sunday morning, etc., about 30 miles each way! The Jacobsons had living quarters in the clubhouse, with an extra bedroom. They offered for me to stay with them many Saturday nights so that my dad would not have to make the extra drives Saturday evenings and Sunday mornings. Golf was a big part of my life all during my jr. high and sr. high school years.

Hours were spent with Bill Shelton on the driving range, first learning how to hit the ball…period, then learning how to hit all kinds of shots. I remember hitting 500 practice shots/day, and then spending an hour or two on the putting green working on putts under 6'. (Since I was the one picking up balls on the driving range as part of my job from 6am to 3pm, and then while I did my own practicing, I was careful to hit balls into a group that made it easier and quicker to pick them up!) In that day, I used an electric golf cart with no roof or protective screen around the driver's seating area, and a 'picker-upper' that Leonard made me: a broom stick cut to my length needed with a Texaco 1 quart oil can (Cynthia's dad was with Texaco!). One end of the can was nailed to the broom stick and the other end completely removed. High tech ball picker-upper! We even went out on the course late Saturday afternoons, and Bill taught me specialty shots to sharpen my short game, sand trap expertise, and learning course management.

I won many junior golf tournaments, and was runner-up in the Texas State Junior Golf Championships in 1962, a tournament sponsored by the San Antonio Light newspaper and played on the old Breckenridge Golf Course near downtown San Antonio. The best junior golfers from all over Texas played there. I lost in the last couple of holes of a 36-hole match-play final to Dave Eichelberger of Waco, who later played on the PGA Tour. I, later, with Henry Ransom as my golf coach and teacher while at Texas A&M University, went back to San Antonio (the week following my marriage to Barbara Becka!), and won the 1967 Texas State Amateur Golf Championship at Pecan Valley CC in San Antonio. Sweet "recovery"!

I won an amateur tourney in Center, Texas in 1966, on the 2nd hole of a playoff with Craig Metz, using a shot Bill Shelton taught me around the green of the 17th hole of Atascocita CC one day. That day in Center was special. My dad and mom were there. My grandfather, O. B. Bradford, we called him Brad, drove over from Commerce to see me play (Is life full of 'ironies'? Brad was an agriculture professor at East Texas State University, now called Texas A&M/Commerce, and Craig was a member of the ETSU golf team...lol!). The shot was almost impossible for someone who had no idea of what to do, or how to do it. But that teaching a few years back came to mind, and I took my sand wedge and made a shot that in my mind was simple. I had done it many times before, and oftentimes dreaming of doing it in a tourney situation! I can picture the course, the shot, my family, and Bill Shelton right now...as if it was yesterday (of course, that was 52 years ago this summer!). My name is on a big sign near the clubhouse with all of that tournament's winners for the past 60 years or so!

Here is an interesting tidbit: those 'used' clubs Bill Shelton grabbed and took to the driving range (they cost us $50 in 1957) that day I first met him, are the same ones I used all through high school and through my first 3 years in college, up to the Center tournament. Winning the Center tourney with THOSE same clubs! In fact, in addition to the 1st place trophy at Center, I won a set of new Spalding Top-Flite irons, and I started using them afterwards. The original Spalding irons my dad had bought me in 1957...the grooves were worn almost completely off on some of the clubs. An interesting footnote: I never spent another dollar on golf clubs my entire life from that first $50 set of used clubs in 1957, EXCEPT my college golf coach, Henry Ransom, SOLD me an old, used persimmon-head driver he had used when he played the PGA Tour and used in winning the 1950 Tam O'Shanter tournament in the Chicago area. He charged me $15 for that club. Until the hosel cracked, I used it to win many tournaments by driving for more than "show"!

Now listen. When I look back on the 30+ years I have pastored, and counseled many as a Life Coach, I always remember the techniques and the principles that correspond in life with biblically-based Truths. This book is all about that. Always remember this: a Truth can have many applications. Truths learned in one area of life can be used in others. But ALL TRUTH comes from God. There is a connection somewhere, somehow, to every Truth in life to the Truth of Life.

Well, what about 2 Timothy 4:7 and Bill's statement about "being so close to the clubhouse"??? Like a flash of lightning, a moment occurred on the first tee of Atascocita Country Club that eventually led to one of the greatest life-changing moments in my life! It was early in the summer of 1960. I had just turned 15 on June 1st. I was participating in a qualifying event for the USGA National Publinx Golf Championship to be played in July that year in Honolulu, Hawaii. Can you imagine the thoughts running through my mind?!? It was a 36-hole event, 2 18-hole rounds of medal play on the same day. I had shot one or two over par in the morning round, and was in contention for one of the three spots to qualify to go to Hawaii. After lunch and warming up for the afternoon round, I was on the first tee to start the afternoon round. Bill Shelton was there. My dad and mom were there. Several friends from the club were there. It came my time to hit. I teed the ball up, took a couple of practice swings, and approached the ball to hit my tee shot. I started my backswing, and just as I was beginning my downswing…BAM! A sudden, startling, loud CRASH of a noise came from my right…about 10 yards away. The fellow who worked with me around the golf shop and golf cart storage shed (we got the golf carts out in the morning, helped players get their bags onto the carts, put the carts up at night… hooking them up to the electric chargers, got members clubs out of the clubhouse storage and out for them to use, and of course, I picked up balls on the driving range in the golf cart with my fantastic "high-tech" ball picker-upper!!!) was hurrying up to the tee in a golf cart to see me hit. He ran into a tree near the tee when the brakes didn't hold well enough! Wow! As I came near making contact with the ball, I flinched or did whatever I did, and what little contact I made with the ball sent it skittering off to the left of the tee among several trees close by. It was a disastrous start to the 2nd round!

Needless to say, I was startled! And flustered. And angry! And I grabbed my bag of clubs and started toward my ball. All sorts of things must have been going through my mind. I don't remember any of the thoughts. I just remember getting to the ball, and having to hit the ball back out toward the fairway only a few yards from the front of the tee. I lay 2, and I am still virtually the whole length of the hole away from the green! It is a par-4 hole. I somehow hit the next shot fairly decently. Then I hit onto the green. Then I 2-putted, for a big, fat double-bogey 6 (that put me as many over par to start the 2nd round as I had finished the first 18 holes!!!). My head was spinning, ugly thoughts running through my mind toward that guy who had hit the tree in a crucial time of my swing, *causing* me to hit the bad shot that led me to the double-bogey. The 25 yard walk from the 1st green to the 2nd tee seemed like eternity. After the others in my group teed off, it was my turn. I teed the ball, took my practice swings, then swang at the ball. You guessed it. It wasn't a *swing*. It was a *swang*. I barely made contact, but fortunately it went straight down the fairway about 100 yards or so. I was still a long way from the 2nd green, this being another par-4 hole.

Now listen, every one of us has moments in life like what happened as I left the 2nd tee. I grabbed my bag, steaming and storming off the tee toward my ball. A golf cart came alongside me. It was Bill Shelton and someone else riding with him (I don't have the slightest remembrance of who was riding with him!). These words came out of Bill's mouth: "Put your clubs on the cart…this is the closest place to the clubhouse. You might as well go in right now." Scouts honor. Honest to God. That's all he said. For me, it was no excuses. Put up or shut up.

I turned and looked him in the face. After who knows how long, I turned back and looked down the fairway toward the 2nd green. Who knows WHY I thought what I thought ("I'm NOT quitting!") or did what I did. But without saying a word, I headed toward my ball. That was some of the most crucial yards I have ever walked in my entire life. In no small way, Bill Shelton took "excuses" out of my vocabulary, and out of my life, which has had a dramatic impact over the years.

All I can say is that I hit a beautiful 2nd shot that got me near the green in an excellent position to hit my 3rd up close to the pin. I made the putt for a par-4, and the rest is history. I played even-par the last 17 holes and qualified for one of the 3 spots to go to Hawaii! The two other guys to qualify that day were men who were well-known to many players around Houston…Lee Pinkston and Tommy Tyson.

Ever since that day in 1960, I have had seemingly innumerable situations where I could have "quit" and not finished. The end results have not always been as positive as that day, but the core value in my life has remained unchanged. After becoming a Christian, I came to identify what God did in my life that day:

61

"I have fought a good fight, I have finished my course,
I have kept the faith." 2 Timothy 4:7

It is one of my *Life verses*.

That moment, that spot not too far in front of the 2nd tee at Atascocita Country Club, and Bill Shelton and that golf cart, are just as vivid in my mind today as if I am standing on the course right now. In fact, only a couple of years ago, Barbara and I were in that area for a friend's 80th birthday – Bill Sevier. He is the man of chapter 13 in this book. Barbara and I drove by and found the green of hole #2 at Atascocita. I got out and stood on that 2nd green and remembered the spot God used Bill Shelton to give me a Life Truth through a practical perspective that has stuck with me to this day.

Thank God for seagulls that cross our path every now and then. Want to know something crazy. Every once in a while back then we would see a seagull in the air over the course at Atascocita, and wonder how in the world they ever got so far away (perhaps 30+ miles) from the salt waters of Galveston and/or Trinity Bay. Seagulls (Truth) can appear anywhere!

I have hanging in my office a picture of Bill Shelton and myself on the practice tee at Atascocita Country Club. It was taken one day when I was back home in Baytown during a break from playing on the PGA Tour. What a privilege to go so far in golf. What a privilege to rub elbows with the greats of professional golf of that day. What a privilege to have had Bill Shelton brought into my life for many reasons, but especially that great life lesson from the 2nd hole at ACC. That picture is a grand reminder of the moment this man impacted my life in a most remarkable way. Who took the picture? My Dad. Immeasurable memory.

Many years later, Bill Shelton came down with cancer. I was fortunate to be called upon by his daughter, Debbie, to tell me of his condition. I went to visit him in a hospital near Humble. Not long after, I officiated his funeral in Humble. Many of those old golf pros Bill used to tell that *his boy* had beaten *their boy* in a jr. golf tournament were there. My dad and mom were there. Cynthia was there. It was a difficult day for us all.

One other footnote: my mom said I was "too young" to go to Hawaii by myself (at age 15), so she and dad scraped the money together for her to go along with me. I've often wondered why I was "too young." I wasn't too young to go by myself to Kansas City, Detroit, or Minneapolis for some USGA and WGA national junior championships…lol!

One final thing: Is an accident that caused me to give up a game I loved as much as any I played (baseball), to meet Bill Shelton and all the others golf brought my way, and to learn one of life's greatest Truths, really that "unfortunate"? I don't think so. This Truth has given me more "grit" than I could have ever imagined. Grit. The stamina of champions.

"Lord Jesus, Thank You for bringing Bill Shelton into my life. I ask for Your grace to continuously be poured out on me so that I can fight the good fight, finish my course, and keep the faith...no matter what trials or tribulations come my way."

Oh, yes...I hope and pray God sends a Bill Shelton into your life at just the right moment! And remember this...Truth will always find a way!

Chapter Seven

Michael Wells – "The nearness of Christ"

"To whom God would make known what is the riches
of the glory of this mystery among the Gentiles;
which is Christ in you, the hope of glory."
Colossians 1:27

Some friends in ministry who lived on a ranch in the Panhandle of Texas called one day back in January, 1998, and asked us to join them for a couples retreat that was going to be during the first week of February (6th-8th) in Colorado. They knew a couple who sponsored a couples retreat every year at a place called Glen Eyrie in Colorado Springs. Glen Eyrie is home to the Navigators' Ministry. Every detail of the place, the people, and the program was enticing. We decided to go.

As time drew near, the planned speaker for the event had to cancel. But the sponsoring couple had another fellow they knew "who just happened to be in the states, was available to come, and agreed to do so." The replacement speaker was Michael Wells. What a huge change was about to come over my life, Barbara's life, even our kids' and grandkids' lives, and many more folks' lives…

The sponsors of the event asked a few pastors and ministry leaders who were attending to read a book by Michael called *Sidetracked in the Wilderness*. We were to read it, meet with Michael shortly before the first session, and be prepared to lead some breakout groups during the conference. What we didn't know was that from the very first moment of meeting and hearing Michael Wells, OUR lives and ministry would never be the same. It was a divine appointment.

Michael, and his wife, Betty, started Abiding Life Ministries International in 1989 as a ministry of encouragement to Believers in many countries. Michael did the teaching and travelling for over 20 years until his death while on mission to Costa Rica in October 2011. Betty was the only "staff" person back home taking care of all office duties, as well as proofing and production of printed materials. Today the ministry is still strong, with the Wells' son, Noah, joining the ministry in their Littleton,

Colorado, office. What makes the ministry so amazing is that there are numerous "partners" around the world doing a "WITH" ministry…each independent of ALMI but joined in presenting the teachings of Michael Wells.

Barbara and I have listened to, read, discussed, and taught so many things that we were exposed to from the ministry of Michael Wells and Abiding Life Ministries International. I want to share a few of the numerous truths that have made us FREE in Christ in the past 20 years.

Michael and ALMI have had one main theme all these years: "There is nothing the nearness of Christ cannot overcome." Michael believed the encouragement he offered comes as we focus on the **Jesus within us**, and as God gives the revelation of **all we possess in Him and Him in us**…that Christian growth is not changing, but involves the revelation of the great exchange (His Life for ours). One simple premise he gave us that grabbed our hearts: "Abiding. Jesus is the Vine, I am just a branch. It's His Life, not mine." (from John 15 teachings) **"There is nothing the nearness of Christ cannot overcome** (cure, change, correct, heal…)" involves being completely aware of Colossians 1:27, "…Christ in you, the hope of glory." Being completely aware of "who we are in Christ." Being completely aware of "Who Christ is in us." Focusing on the Christ in us, and trusting in Him to do for us whatever we need. This is the foundation for overcoming anything life brings our way.

The following are quotations from Michael Wells' *My Weakness for His Strength* book. (used by permission of ALMI). I like to call it his "workbook" on the Abiding Life:

"Abiding"…p.3, 229 in MWfHS

Every vine preaches and teaches Jesus. Abiding is the culmination of His work and is everything, for in abiding we receive the Everything, Jesus. Is it not amazing that the whole work of Jesus is revealed in this one word?

Abiding: holding me in Him, His life in me, cleansing, revealing what I am, kept safe from so much disease, a moment-by-moment existence, eternal life.

"Jesus is The Vine, I am just a branch."…p.131 in MWfHS

Abide in Christ and all that He is and has is received, just as the branch receives the full life of the vine. Do not abide and immediately experience being in the flesh.

"It's Him, not me."…p.236-237 in MWfHS

A believer will do so much by doing nothing!

As a branch the believer is unique and independent but must use the freedom to choose to do nothing unless the Lord is doing it through him. The believer needs to see he is in control of his actions, and the action he needs to take is inviting Jesus to come and soak him and be his life in the present situation. In the end he will have an expression of Christ through him that is not he.

"True vs Truth." …p.246-247 in MWFHS

Not everything that is true is truth. A teaching may come from Scripture and be true but not truth.

True teaching that lands at our feet and speaks of what we must do is not truth. True teaching that ends at the feet of Jesus and explains what He does for us is truth.

If what we are hearing does not land at His feet, it is not truth.

What does land at our feet is the issue of our being unbelieving toward having a deep, personal relationship with Jesus and continuing to maintain that there is something lacking that I must do or find.

Lesser vs Greater…p.298 in MWfHS

Lesser truth must always give way to greater truth…every believer must be careful not to worship a lesser truth but allow the lesser truth to bring him to the greatest truth. We can run the risk of worshiping and serving something created rather than the Creator.

I once read a list of what it means to live in self-denial (long list given). The problem was that self-denial was portrayed as the greater truth.

As we fellowship with Christ, all the above that needs to happen does happen.

God is always to be the focus, and to the surprise of many, there are elements of self with which today He is not concerned about dealing. We must make the greater truth our focus, and then we may be assured that all lesser truth will not be neglected.

Believing before doing…p.268, 37 in MWfHS

Doing makes the Christian life far too difficult! It is not the doing that must come first but the believing.

The beginning in God's order is abiding! How do we abide? He has put us in Him, He holds us in Him, and it is His life flowing though us. The emphasis is not on us but on Him, for He has done it all. Only believe it, confess it, and acknowledge it. Once our focus is on Him, His life flows, we bear fruit--the end result of the proper order--and the Father is glorified. It is His doing.

Unbelief measured by the number of our questions...p.121 in MWfHS

I have often thought that theology is a course of study for the unbelieving Believer, a man with an I.Q. of 150 attempting to understand a God with an immeasurably infinite I.Q. In the West we have developed an unhealthy fascination with questioning and understanding God. Unbelief can be measured in direct proportion to the number of our questions...

Living to man...p.312 in MWfHS

Living to and for men is one of the worst kinds of bondage, for anyone living to man cannot live to God, the Giver of freedom.

There are several ways to live for man: giving glory, taking glory, giving judgment, receiving judgment, showing partiality because of worldly resources, groveling at the image or position of "greatness," discussing man's "secret" failings, refusing to ask a question, avoiding a confrontation, or reacting to criticism. I have done it all, and I tell you it is a miserable way to live.

There is another way to live, free from man-pleasing; however, this freedom comes through faith. We must believe completely and unreservedly that we have a God who provides for us in every way, financially, physically, emotionally, and spiritually. We must believe that He opens doors, provides the way, and gives us wisdom. We must believe that He gives us everything needed, and that in Him we will find everything that we have looked for elsewhere in vain. For it is only in seeing that God meets all of our needs that frees us from the root of living for men, that root being the belief that man can provide something that we need. If assurance, significance, value, and worth come from God, what does man have to offer? If man has nothing to provide that we need-no praise, position, or possession--then we are free not to live to man. Again, living for the approval of man has at its root the belief that man can give us something that God will not.

Life...p.119, 247, 305, 308-309 in MWfHS

The believer has a new birth, a new life that has dealt a fatal deathblow to self; because of this death he can have Life.

Experiencing God could not be more than what He has given us as individuals to experience...we are pleasing and close to Him because the life of Christ in us is pleasing and close.

The only thing that is natural for man is the absolute of Christ, for He created and holds man together. Hence, He is the Way!

God is the Author of life, and for life to run smoothly, it must run in Him.

When it comes to our life in Christ, we do not need a better education; we need revelation. Jesus reveals to us the limitation of an education. Only the Holy Spirit brings revelation.

Focus on Christ...p.530-531 in MWfHS

Michael used one particular illustration often when speaking. He would hold his left hand up in front of him and say this hand was "problems." He would draw the hand closer to his face and speak of how the problems got "bigger" in his sight. Then Michael would take his right hand and put it out in front of him and say this hand was "Jesus." Then he would take his left hand and put it "behind" his right hand. Michael then pointed out that when his right hand (Jesus) was all he could see (because it had hidden his left hand) his problems had diminished. However, he would swap positions with his hands...and his "problems" were "hiding Jesus." Wherever his focus was, whatever was closest to his "sight," THAT dominated his life. Focusing on Jesus dominated over problems. He would then tell everyone: "Do not let Jesus be anything but all you are focusing on."

If Truth can set anyone free for five minutes, then it can set him free for a lifetime. Truth is absolute and therefore cannot go off and on like a light switch.

Truth is something to be walked in as faith works alongside to bring experience. Faith allows us to receive the Truth and walk in it. Those who tell me that focusing on Christ does not work are never focusing on Christ while they make that statement. To know the power of truth one must walk in it, and I have never had anyone that was abiding in Christ tell me that it did not work.

When we decide to not walk in Truth we rebel, and the one thing that will most facilitate rebellion and render us the least uncomfortable during the process is anger. The process is 1) rebel, 2) develop anger, and 3) justify the anger.

Believer, YOU CHOOSE! Your will is not broken. John 15 is Truth; walk in it and it will once again prove its power to you to the point that you will shout, "It works!"

Our journey with Michael Wells has been a wonderful one, full of God and His grace. It was our great pleasure and privilege to host Michael for a conference in the church I was pastoring in Houston back in the late 1990's. We also were able to see him at conferences in Conroe, Tomball, and Georgetown (all Texas towns). We participated in a workshop at a retreat center in Oklahoma. I was privileged to be a part of a Men's Retreat in the mountains west of Colorado Springs…two different ones, in fact. Michael Wells was the same man in the "pulpit" that he was at the restaurant, on the porch, or in the car. His message was always the same.

Barbara and I spent a couple of days with Betty at their home west of Pueblo in 2014. And what a joy and privilege to take a day to journey with Betty to the cabin in the mountains west of there where Michael spent so much time with God, doing much meditating and writing. But, just the time with Betty was special. We had first met her at the Couples Retreat in Colorado back in 1998. We still have contact and interaction with Betty to this day, and Betty is the same "at the office" (however and wherever that works out to be!) as she is in her home, driving through the mountains, or walking their property down by the creek below their home.

As only God could design, Barbara and I just stayed with Betty in her new place in Littleton, as she had moved back into the office there in recent days. Once again, the moments were special. And we got to meet Noah, his wife and kids, and eat a meal with them. In addition, Tim Lester (from Maryland) was there preparing with Noah for another one of those fabulous men's retreats that was soon approaching. Paths crossing, time spent in special Christian fellowship, and Truth being shared is one way God gives each of us a hint of all that He is doing in this small world.

Barbara and I thank God for giving us Michael and Betty Wells to be a part of our lives, and ultimately part of our entire family's lives. ALMI has been a major part of our growth in Life as a Christian. And the Truth of "Christ in me" has been the power of my life the past 20 years.

Let me encourage you to get in contact with Betty Wells at ALMI and see about how to get some of their books, materials, items on website, etc.

Abiding Life Ministries International
P.O. Box 620998, Littleton, CO 80162
303-972-0859
www.abidinglife.com
facebook: abidinglife

"Lord Jesus, Thank You for blessing us with Michael and Betty Wells. You have given us great revelation through ALMI's teachings that speak Truth, and You reveal what is Truth to us. You are Truth. Thank You for the awesome Truth that You live inside me! Your Life MAKES living Life as a Christian so uncomplicated, so comfortable, and so peaceful. I rest and focus on You, Lord Jesus."

Oh, yes…I hope and pray God sends a Michael Wells (and a Betty) into your life at just the right moment! And remember this…Truth will always find a way!

Chapter Eight

Gary & Anne Marie Ezzo – "We're the Davises…"

"Train up a child in the way he should go: and
when he is old, he will not depart from it."
Proverbs 22:6

One evening in May in the 1990's, at a doctor's house near Conroe,
Texas, God intervened at a meeting of folks interested in Gary and Anne
Marie Ezzo's ministry to parents, Growing Families.Life. (There is a lot
more about their ministry at the end of this chapter!). We were gathered
to meet the Ezzos and learn what their teaching might do to help us help
parents. My wife and I, and others from our church, were convinced at
what we heard. And Barbara and I went on to teach the Ezzo's workshop
(then called *Growing Kids God's Way*) several times. Some in our first
gathering have gone on to teach it in other churches, in other states. All
have shared the truths again and again as they have seen God do some
marvelous work in their family's life. But the evening proved once again
that God has more in store than first meets the eye. If you look closely,
when God is at work, so many times seagulls are around somewhere…
and never forget, s*eagulls don't lie!*

For one thing the couples we have been involved with have
continued over the years to be faithful friends and dedicated parents.
Their families alone are one of the grandest testimonies of the years we
have spent in ministry. You will hear from two or three of them in the
16th chapter of this book.

However, at one point in the evening of that couple's beautiful back
yard in the Woodlands area, something about fishing came up. You can
imagine what that led to! From that moment on, Gary Ezzo became a
special friend. And our paths would cross in more casual gatherings in
each other's homes, in the waters of Texas and South Carolina, as well as
church settings. But what I want to emphasize, in the midst of that
friendship, is the numerous Truths from God that the Ezzos shared with
us about training up a child God's Way, and what we today continue to

share with couples who want to listen and learn what God can do in their family.

It is incredible, really, that a couple can become parents without ANY learning, training, equipping, coaching, and most likely…never knowing what God has to say in His Word about parenting. And how did GOD get removed from the equation?!? *Gary and Anne Marie Ezzo have brought God back into parents' lives in a big and beautiful way!*

It has been the McDowell's privilege to host Gary and Anne Marie in our home, and to be their guest in their home. They are beautiful people. They have been gifted by God to share and work with couples all over the world. I have contacted the Ezzos to get their permission to use extensive quotes of their teachings in this writing. What I share is by no means more than just a *small smidgeon* of what you can gain from them. These are my idea of "highlights" that I have seen work, and are still working for 1,000's of families.

First of all, I used to do a short "parenting workshop" in our church in Houston for parents whose kids came to our Vacation Bible School. The parents could bring their young kids for VBS, stay and gain valuable info from the workshop, then be there at the closing ceremony to gather their kid(s) and leave. The parents loved this plan. (Keep in mind, these were parents who did not attend our church). So, I called it the "Top 10 Tips For Parenting," and I covered 2 each night. Total credit was given to the Ezzos for the material I was teaching. See if any of these titles interest you and could possibly help you! You will find them in the Ezzos' materials:

1. Training the Heart

2. The Father's Mandate

3. Our Moral Warehouse

4. "Life Is Not Fair"

5. R-E-S-P-E-C-T

6. "Red Cup, Blue Cup"

7. The Interrupt Rule

8. The Appeal Process

9. "We're working on that."

10. "We're the Davises…"

I will discuss #10 in more detail with a beautiful illustration. It has proven to be one of the most effective, simplistic teachings a parent can get into their kid's mind with dramatic results...

One more item that I was reminded of recently. In their GKGW classes the Ezzos taught us an action for the family that got my attention. It was their session on "Memorials." Gary and Anne Marie pointed out that when a major event has occurred, and God has shown Himself strong on your behalf (especially with your kids, or the family as a whole), set aside something that can serve as a "memorial" that can remind you and your family members of when God worked grace in your life.

I am a big autograph getter, ticket collector (not speeding, etc.!), and items from events or people that remind me of the moments they were obtained. I like thinking back to those times. So, it didn't surprise me when Barbara and I were watching a Hallmark movie last Christmas and one of the characters said, "These ornaments are memories on branches." They were talking about their favorite tree ornaments that someone made for them or gifted them with in past years. Some had hung on the family's Christmas tree for many, many years. We both turned to each other and said, "the Ezzos!"

One interesting personal note about the Ezzos. They are coffee aficionados! They have even impacted how the McDowells drink coffee! Today, Barbara and I drink certain coffees, and measure the grounds to be brewed with the special silver "scoop" the Ezzos gave us as a gift (over 20 years ago!) after staying in our home one time. Other than being a parenting and coffee aficionado, Gary is also a fishing expert.

Oh, yes, I couldn't write about Gary and Anne Marie without a fishing story...

On one occasion when the Ezzos came to Houston for a visit, Gary and I went fishing in East Matagorda Bay. Barbara and Anne Marie and some ladies from our church went shopping and antiquing. Bruce Baugh had loaned Gary and me his boat. We were excited about getting into those trout-infested waters. It was a fabulous day on the water...not! The wind started howling, and we started looking for anywhere we could find clear water in a wind-protected area. Seems like we wandered all over the strangest places hoping to find a place to fish. After perhaps the worst day ever, we headed back to the marina, loaded the boat, and headed back home. However, as usual, we stopped at a Whataburger to grab one of those fabulous Texas hamburgers that the great baseball icon Nolan Ryan once proclaimed: "Whataburger, it's what a burger ought to be!" Gary loves those Texas Whataburgers!

73

So, the day wasn't a complete bust. And especially so, as we were driving up Hwy 288 from Lake Jackson, I asked Gary an impromptu question: "Gary, in all your years of writing, speaking, preaching and teaching about parenting, kids, being a Dad and Mom...what do you think might be the most important truth of all you've taught?" I added, "Is that a fair question? Is it possible to narrow all you teach down to one or two 'most important' truths?" He spoke without hardly a pause: "The two greatest issues for kids: (1) they can't emotionally handle being 'boss.' And, (2) they can't handle sexual issues at such an early age." The Ezzos' teaching on "Innocence" is an impressive admonition for parents to follow.

I was amazed at the comprehensive, complex issues that those two statements spoke to. Gary did a lot of explaining in the next several minutes (his and Anne Marie's materials cover these in great detail... see bottom of this chapter for info on contacting them, and procuring their materials), but I have to tell you that I have thought about those two things, shared them numerous times, and still today (again, at least 20 years later) have seen his comments proved over and over again in the lives of kids and parents I have pastored, or observed at the local grocery or Walmart. Two statements. Two different realms of the life of kids, parents, and parenting. But the impact involving no telling how many lives (perhaps entire countries) is evident everywhere I go... church, grocery store, restaurants, Walmart, ball games...everywhere! It is staggering the number of times I am reminded of that simple little moment when the man I most respect as God's servant to teach and aid parents all over the world in "training up a child in the way he should go" so quickly, so simply, so confidently shared two of life's greatest ills in the world of bearing and rearing children. Gary's famous "Red cup, blue cup" story is detailed in the "Top 10" list above, and suffice it to say he leaves parents stunned in their seats when they hear him speak of just why they are having such difficulty with their kids obeying them.

Well, let me close this tribute to the Ezzos by speaking to the title of this chapter: Gary & Anne Marie Ezzo – "We're the Davises..." One of the first couples we had going through the GKGW course was Brian and Jill Davis. Brian and I became friends when his wife visited the church I was pastoring in west Houston back in the mid-90's, and she said, "My husband doesn't go to church anymore. He got thrown out of our last church in Virginia. He is a disc jockey and the preacher said he couldn't belong and play the devil's music on the radio." That was like waving a red flag in front of this bull. Off to the Davis home I go! Since that first meeting, Brian and I have been best friends. In fact, I still today call him "my best friend." Barbara and I have travelled all over America to visit the Davis family, as Brian was moved by the radio business he works in (different stations in Richmond, Virginia; Seattle, Washington; Wichita, Kansas; and now Norfolk/Virginia Beach, Virginia). Brian and Jill have two wonderful daughters…today, grown and married with young children. Allison and Sarah (and their spouses) are teaching their kids what Brian and Jill taught them. Brian and Jill's daughters were ages 5 and 3 when they first came to our church in Houston.

Not too long after going through the GKGW class, Brian shared a really beautiful story with me as we were "walk-jogging" in the predawn hours in their neighborhood (too long of a story to describe right now…contact me for this great exercise method!). Brian said to me, "Just last night Jill and I were talking with the girls about something one of their friends was doing that we thought inappropriate for our girls to do. Out of the blue, the girls say, 'Daddy, WE'RE THE DAVISES, aren't we…we don't do those things!'" Wow! Just one small tip Gary and Anne Marie tell parents to teach their kids. One giant Truth that grips the heart of two small young children so much more than any scolding, or even perhaps any discipline. Family identity. Belonging to the family. Part of the family with Dad and Mom and siblings. Let me repeat: this has proven to be one of the most effective, simplistic teachings a parent can get into their kid's mind with dramatic results. The impact is just as powerful as the "We're working on that!" Impact, strong, gripping, "home"-changing. Well, amen!

Let me encourage you with all my heart to get into the Growing Families.Life family of blessed parents (and grandparents!) all around the world! It is with great joy that I encourage and recommend everything the Ezzos have available to parents. Their grouping of materials is large. Virtually the parenting of every age of a child is covered. Here is the current information for you to contact the Ezzos, find out more about Growing Families.Life, check out materials available (and order), find out about gatherings where the Ezzos are speaking, discover local classes available where parents meet with leaders who guide through a study (with personal encouragement and answering of questions), and find ways you and your family can be encouraged and have an enhanced life through this vibrant global ministry. All Ezzo curricula is now online and can be streamed for free. Find it at:

www.GrowingFamilies.Life
Growing Families.Life (facebook)
growingfamilieslife (Instagram)
GrowingFamilies.Life (Twitter)

And by the way, if you are anywhere near the coast and see some seagulls circling, look close to see if you don't spot Gary Ezzo casting into the midst of those gulls. He has more fishing licenses for different states than most golfers have golf clubs in their bags!

"Heavenly Father, thank You for bringing Gary and Anne Marie Ezzo into my life. The same Truths that you gave me through them have had an enormous impact on people around the world. Only You know the extent of what I am saying. Thank You for Your power, Your provision, Your promotion, and Your protection of families that are desiring to follow Your wisdom in the Holy Scriptures. Thank You for working in Gary and Anne Marie Ezzo's lives to bring about their global ministry to parents. We want and need all of You and Your Truth that we can receive to see You Live through parents who are available to You. Come be the Divine Parent guiding and living through the earthly parents in Your family."

Oh, yes…I hope and pray God sends Gary & Anne Marie Ezzo into your life at the opportune moment! And remember this…Truth will always find a way!

Chapter Nine

Charles Stanley – "The Eternal Security of Every Believer"

"I give unto them eternal life; and they shall never perish,
neither shall any man pluck them out of my hand."
John 10:28

It would probably take a few books to put down all the things I have learned from Dr. Charles Stanley, Pastor of the 1ˢᵗ Baptist Church, Atlanta, Georgia. Many years of listening to him on radio/television/cassette tapes/cds/and in person, reading his books, and receiving his monthly In Touch magazines have given me multitudes of insights into God and God's Truths. It has been my privilege to meet him briefly on a couple of occasions.

Barbara and I for years would have our clock radio set to sound the alarm and start broadcasting around 5:50am…time to turn the coffee on, and get a hot cup, before Charles Stanley's daily radio broadcast came on. Over and over we would be blessed with that familiar delivery of, "Now, listen…" I loved it. I picked up that habit several years ago!

I can close my eyes and see the seagulls circling while Charles Stanley's voice sounds in my ears…Truth is about to be known. There are a couple of things I remember the most about his delivery:

1. Charles Stanley always delivers Truth from God's Word

2. Charles Stanley always is precise and pointed in giving Truth

3. Charles Stanley always explains and illustrates the Truths given

4. Charles Stanley always calls for a response to Truth received

It didn't matter the subject, Charles Stanley gave God's supply for whatever our need was. I learned from him early on to enumerate and categorize the points of my message to help the people to grasp and better understand the Truths and their application. I have always thought of Charles Stanley as a preacher's preacher, or a pastor's pastor.

Perhaps one of the first great Truths I learned in great detail from Charles Stanley was this: every Believer's salvation is eternally secure. The following are my notes I took from listening to Dr. Stanley's message on "The Eternal Security of Every Believer":

> Eternal security is that work of God by which He guarantees that the gift of salvation, once received, is forever possessed and cannot be lost. It is not on the basis of a Believer's performance, not on the basis of behavior, not on the basis of conduct, not on the basis of any promises to do good…but on the basis that God has made a promise in the person of Jesus Christ.

Wow! Hallelujah!

1. John 10:27-30 – the personal promise of Jesus Christ.

> a promise with no conditions attached to it.
> we are His sheep, He knows us.
>
> Matthew 7:21 – "I never knew you." If works and miracles could get us to heaven, these folks would be there. Jesus was telling them "I never knew you as a true believer of Me."
>
> it is a quality of Life…His Life it is a
> quantity of Life…Eternal Life
>
> they shall never perish…there are no conditions added.
> no one shall ever snatch them out of My hand…they can never be lost.
>
> Psalm 89:13 – hand of God. the hand of omnipotence and omniscience.
>
> My Father has given them unto Me. And no one is able to snatch them out of My Father's hand. I and My Father are one. That is what Jesus said.
>
> If a person can be saved and then lost, Jesus has made a promise He cannot deliver.
> If a person can be saved and then lost, there would be some power in this world more powerful than the Omnipotent God, the Omnipotent Son, the Omnipotent Spirit.
> Can you believe what Jesus said? That's the choice.

(I wonder why Dr. Stanley didn't add…"*Seagulls Don't Lie!*" Neither can God.)

2. Hebrews 7:25 - the continuing intercession of Jesus on our behalf

He not only saves us, but He continually watches over us and maketh intercession for us.

Romans 8:34
1 John 2:1
No matter what happens in our life, Jesus – the nail-scarred Savior – is there to plead our cause. All sins – past, present, future – have been placed on Him. He declares our righteousness on the basis of His blood He shed for us. He knows our failures, He knows our faults, He knows our moments of doubt, He knows our moments of unbelief… and He has forgiven us all these.

John 17:11, 15 – would Jesus Christ ever make a prayer to the Father that He knew the Father would not keep? No!

Hebrews 7:25 – He is able to save us forever, to the uttermost.

Jesus is continually interceding on our behalf.

3. Romans 8:31 - our inseparable relationship with Christ

the atoning death of Jesus Christ has secured and sealed our relationship with Him. once we have been saved, we are secure for all eternity.

on the basis of God's justifying power, we arc declared not guilty…we cannot be condemned because we have already been declared righteous in the eyes of God.

it is the work of Christ, not our work. the atoning work of Christ would be only temporary if I could lose what the shedding of His blood did for me, and all the rest of the world.
Romans 8:33-39
God gives us three questions, and then tells us His answers:
Who shall lay any thing to the charge of God's elect?

No one. It is God that justifieth.

The only one who tries is the devil, but he cannot.

Who is he that condemneth?

No one. It is Christ who maketh intercession for us.

Who/what shall separate us from the love of Christ?

No one. Nothing. (God gives us 5 verses full of 17 things – events, experiences, time, persons, powers, place, anything created that CANNOT separate us from the LOVE OF GOD IN CHRIST JESUS)

The grace of God was not offered on the basis of my performing, my keeping on living up to…but my sin debt has been paid no matter what happens.

You and I can be absolutely confident that we are absolutely secure in Christ. Saved forever, by the grace of God. Once possessed, it is yours forever…it cannot be lost.

Eternal Security.

I love Dr. Stanley's preaching. Seagulls flying everywhere, all the time!

This truth is one of the most important truths to convey to every new Believer soon after their New Birth. All sorts of events, experiences, time, persons, powers, places, and things will try to steal away a Believer's security. Especially that of a new Believer.

Just how important is it to you that you have the security of knowing that your eternal future is sound, sealed, and secure? Anyone who has ever been Born Again has been confronted with questions, perhaps doubts, and thoughts about this issue.

Dr. Hal Boone, Minister of Missions at Sagemont Church years ago, once told me that only those who have been Born Again will ever "doubt" whether they have been saved. But those doubts and questions can make one's spiritual life miserable and less effective (no peace, no comfort, no joy). It is the eternal Word of God that brings the God of peace and the peace of God to our hearts, along with the comfort of Holy Spirit's presence.

I remember the first time I was privileged to hear Charles Stanley in person. It was in January, 1985. It was in the 1st Baptist Church, Euless, Texas. Jimmy Draper was the pastor. It was a *Real Evangelism Conference.* Bailey Smith and John McKay were the evangelistic team of Real

Evangelism. Joe Simmons was their "front man" (the man behind the scenes, the man doing most of the "leg work"). A lady named Reba was their piano player. John could twitch his nose one direction or the other and Reba would know what song he wanted to do next! Interestingly, I had been the Bus Minister/Minister of Evangelism at Sagemont Church in Houston under Pastor John Morgan (who was a long-time friend of Smith's and McKay's, and Joe was a member at Sagemont). I had been knowing God wanted me to go into the pastorate, and Joe Simmons had a place near Sattler (the small town just below the dam at Canyon Lake). There was a new church there looking for their first pastor. Somehow, they got my name and invited me to come out to meet with the Pastor Search Committee, then later to come back and preach in view of a "call." I became the 1st pastor at Cranes Mill Baptist Church in late December, 1984, with my first Sunday in the pulpit the first Sunday of January, 1985. It was 3 weeks later that Barbara and I went to the *Real Evangelism Conference* in Euless.

As was my custom, I wanted to sit on the front row to hear the great messengers that were arranged to speak. Some folks say they don't want to sit down close in case the preacher gives out some saliva every now and then. But me, I wanted it to get all over me! At that conference one night, my pastor, John Morgan, invited me and Barbara to go with him to John McKay's home for supper. There were 10-15 of the preachers there! Unbelievable! Us and these great men in the home of the McKays at the same moment!

Well, back to Charles Stanley and the conference. I was thinking that I might have a note in one of my old bibles (as my habit has been for years) of the scripture and date that Dr. Stanley spoke one night. You aren't going to believe this. I could hardly believe it myself. In my first "study" and "reference" bible I ever had after being Born Again, The Open Bible – Authorized KJV edition, I found the text for Stanley's message: John 8:28-36. Can you believe it?!? Seagulls were circling and diving right in front of me before I had even heard of such! I underlined two verses while Dr. Stanley preached...v.32, "And ye shall know the truth, and the truth shall make you free," and v.36, "If the Son therefore shall make you free, ye shall be free indeed." WOW! The text that later God has used to put this book together!

Now, listen! I don't remember the title, the outline, the whole of the message from that sermon, but I do remember I went away with a magnanimous truth that I needed in my first month of pastoring! You see, I had been under attack from two of the members who had voted against my becoming the first pastor of Cranes Mill only 1 month before (the vote had been 119-4 in favor of my call. I didn't know it at the time, but the four who voted "no" took our family to lunch after the service!!!). Their story is a long one, and I can't even take a moment to get into it. But suffice it to say, I faced an ordeal that first-time pastors (no, NO pastor) should ever face. What Charles Stanley said in his message that carried me through the next 6 months was this: "Preacher, sometimes you will face challenges and attacks from some in your congregation that they themselves don't even know why they are doing what they are doing. They are so bound up with anger, hurt, pain, unforgiveness, and ultimately, bitterness, they lash out at anything that has anything to do with God. Now listen," Dr. Stanley said, "these people have always had something tragic and/or very grievous happen in their lives. They 'blame' God but find out no matter how much or how hard they 'swing' out against God, they can't hit Him. So, they turn to their pastor, their church, something that has something to do with God, and start swinging away! They are very destructive people." Then Stanley said this, "Keep walking with God. He will bring Truth to bear. He will bring Jesus into the situation." Without giving any of the details, I tell you God did just that, and all was over in a few months. But not without some others who were close friends of that couple joining them in their war against me, other leaders, and the entire church. God showed His faithfulness to deliver us from their evil ways.

I don't remember seeing any actual seagulls flying and circling around Canyon Lake back in 1985, but I can tell you there have been many (a whole lot!) times since I met Bruce Baugh that I have thought of just how Truth won out, the 'liar birds' didn't. And I have never forgotten that moment in that *Real Evangelism Conference* when I heard Dr. Stanley give me a Truth from Truth Himself.

But, again, isn't it incredible that 33 years later, I look in that old bible and find the text of Charles Stanley's message on January 25, 1985, fits like a good pair of work boots (as we country people say) for a prime part in this book of honor. A book to honor God and His Word. A book to honor God and His faithfulness to His Word. A book to honor people like Dr. Charles Stanley who have spoken Truth, and I would imagine to this day he doesn't know the impact in many lives in Texas that his words of 1/25/85 have had.

Of course, my recollection here is smaller than the smallest proverbial needle in the haystack of life where Charles Stanley and his In Touch Ministries have impacted so many millions around the world. But as you go on in life from this time forward, keep looking for the birds that are working in your life. The seagulls that do not lie. The Truth that MAKES you free!

I have several books written by Dr. Stanley. Among those I recommend you obtain:

Forgiveness
A Touch of His Wisdom
A Touch of His Love
A Touch of His Freedom
A Touch of His Peace
Confronting Casual Christianity
A Man's Touch

The Source of My Strength (this one is perhaps the closest to a lengthy personal testimony of Dr. Stanley's life as a Christian…it is FABULOUS info about this great man!)

And anytime you can listen to Dr. Stanley on the radio or television, through his In Touch Ministries program, I heartedly recommend it!

"Lord Jesus, thank You for bringing Dr. Charles Stanley into my life. Thank You that millions of folks around the world have been recipients of Truth because of what You have shared through Dr. Stanley. Thank You for always bringing to sight You and Your Truth. And, to show your Saints the lie. May You show Yourself plain and clear, precise and complete, each and every time we need Truth."

Oh yes, I pray that God sends Dr. Charles Stanley your way at that precise moment you need to hear a Word from God! And remember this…Truth will always find a way!

Chapter Ten

Bruce Wilkinson – "The Testing of Your Faith"

"Now the just shall live by faith: but if any man draw back, my soul shall have no pleasure in him." Hebrews 10:38

You may recognize the name of Bruce Wilkinson from his hugely popular book: *The Prayer of Jabez*. Or, perhaps another popular book he wrote: *Secrets of The Vine*. He is also well-known from his *Walk Thru the Bible Ministries* he founded in 1976. I first got a glimpse of God speaking through him when I picked up his book called: *Experiencing Spiritual Breakthroughs, the Three Chairs*. This book explains, in my mind at least, the primary reason far too many Christian parents fail to see their children follow the parent's footsteps in a living faith of the Lord Jesus Christ.

It has been my privilege to meet Dr. Bruce Wilkinson, and to discover a 12-session study he titled "The Testing of Your Faith." I once told him I thought his study was the greatest bible study course ever done. One reason is because it is done on "faith." Without which God has told us it is impossible to please Him. To me that alone makes it a candidate for one of the greatest teachings. The other reason I gave Dr. Wilkinson is because he lays out a huge number of clear and uncomplicated Truths from God's Word which show us exactly HOW, WHY, WHEN and for WHOSE benefit all the "tests" are given. Way too many Christians do everything they can to <u>avoid</u> God's tests of their faith (we will explore that more in just a moment). That is sad, because God says He gives us tests to prove we have HIS genuine biblical Faith, and they are for OUR benefit (and they can benefit us in a grand way!).

Let me include for just a moment some of my most favorite verses containing the word "faith": by the way, have you ever noticed in a concordance that the English word "faith" appears ONLY two (2) times in the Old Testament AND two-hundred forty-nine (249) times in the New Testament...interesting. That actually speaks volumes to us.

Hebrews 11:6, "But without faith it is impossible to please Him: for he that cometh to God must believe that He is, and that He is a rewarder of them that diligently seek Him."

Hebrews 11:1, "Now faith is the substance of things hoped for, the evidence of things not seen."

Galatians 2:16, "Knowing this that a man is not justified by the works of the law, but by the faith of Jesus Christ, even we have believed in Jesus Christ, that we might be justified by the faith of Christ, and not by works of the law: for by the works of the law shall no flesh be justified."

Galatians 2:20, "I am crucified with Christ: nevertheless I live; yet not I, but Christ liveth in me: and the life which I now live in the flesh I live by the faith of the son of God."

Habakkuk 2:4, "…the just shall live by his faith."

Romans 1:17, "…the just shall live by faith."

Galatians 5:22, "But the fruit of the Spirit is love, joy, peace, longsuffering, gentleness, goodness, faith…"

Romans 10:17, "So then faith cometh by hearing, and hearing by the word of God."

I could go on and on listing verse after verse of great Truth given by God about "His faith." I would encourage you to seek out and find those verses that God would grant to you to become what I call LIFE VERSES, verses that are real in your life…you own them, they "dictate" your actions because God has talked you into their content and no one can talk you out of them.

One of my most favorite statements Dr. Wilkinson has made about the testing of our faith: "Our faith is being tested more than anything else in our life while we are on this earth. Not whether we have sin in our life, or not whether we have fruit/good works…"

This and the many other words God has given him for this particular study have convinced me that this is a study EVERY Christian should go through time and time again.

So, I want to share some of the best truths that Dr. Wilkinson draws our attention to: (these are not direct quotes, but they are accurately drawn directly from his series. And as a matter of interest, my wife and I have watched Dr. Wilkinson's video study many, many times. And I have written down almost 300 "important truths" in my workbook. It was really difficult to choose which ones to include in this writing. I FOLLOW EACH WITH PERSONAL COMMENTS.)

God doesn't tell us in advance of a test.

Isn't that interesting. But, actually, if it is going to be a test of whether or not we HAVE His faith, it must be a test that comes without notice.

We will be tested many times.

One of the most difficult realities Christians have to face: there is not just ONE test of our faith in life. There will be many. Actually, until we "pass" one test, we will continue to be tested on that same issue until we pass.

We can be tested in many different ways.

The "ways" of testing might be infinite. But each test is designed by God just for us as one of His children. The number of ways is not important, but recognizing the different ways as a test from God is what is important.

God is in control of our tests and knows all that is going on.

Christians like to boast about our God being "in control." But let a test of our faith come along and notice how quick we can speak and act like God has totally lost control. How sad. One minute we say we know and have God; the next minute we are living as if we don't.

Each test is about what I believe about God.

THIS could be the most telling aspect of each test. WHAT do I BELIEVE about God? Do I believe He is omnipotent, omniscient, and omnipresent? Do I believe He can be trusted to do as He says? Do I believe He will be faithful? Now, listen, the amount of faith that you and I have and live by is the sum of what we believe about God and His faithfulness.

God never expects us to fail a test of our faith.

Never. God's history is flawless. That's His history from the day He created Adam & Eve. That's His history with us. This is one of the most profound and impactful Truths Bruce Wilkinson confronts us with! God EXPECTS us to PASS EVERY test of our faith He allows our way. IF we would simply BELIEVE GOD and HIS

WORD, there is not one test life could bring our way that we would not pass. Such a word is Romans 8:28. Or, Hebrews 13:5. Or, Proverbs 3:5-6. Or, Philippians 4:13, 19. I have over 500 of these verses. Contact me if you need some words of God for you to start BELIEVING GOD.

We are known for having wrong responses to God's testing. (Dr. Wilkinson gives "5 Wrong Responses" in his study) These wrong responses involve compromising our faith, verbally complaining about our circumstances, criticizing people in charge, getting angry with God, and corrupting other believer's faith. Just to hear Dr. Wilkinson working through these can bring chills to hearts that are not trusting God.

Very often we fail a test because we are unaware of what the Bible teaches the test is about.

(that's a sad indictment on us, isn't it?) One of Dr. Wilkinson's most incredible, eye-opening statements: "**God teaches to the test!**" That one alone will throw a lot of modern-day educators into a tailspin! The gall of a teacher to do that! <u>Much</u> <u>less</u> <u>God</u>. Well, God precedes every test of our faith with teaching us in a way that we can trust Him when the test arrives. Don't miss this!

God is teaching us before He tests us.

We can know when we are in a test of our faith.

Dr. Wilkinson speaks of "feelings" that surface when we are in a test of our faith.

1 Peter 1:7 tells us that a purpose of the trial of our faith "might be found unto praise and honor and glory at the appearing of Jesus Christ." Wilkinson says that when we feel anger, impatience, or irritation, they indicate a first reaction to a test of faith. Discouragement is another feeling that may come. Let me insert a personal observation from over the years: these feelings tie right into Proverbs 12:25, "Heaviness (or anxiety) in the heart of man maketh it stoop (or, causeth depression), but a good word maketh it glad." Negative emotions means I don't believe the truth of a situation. I am believing a lie. Anger means "I want to be in control." When I believe what I should believe, that which could cause me to negatively respond doesn't occur any more! Listen to Dr. Wilkinson: "A test of my faith is not about how I will act, but what I believe. No one has a problem with their temper...but with their faith."

If we increase what we believe about God, we will act appropriately during a test.

If we could call something the "key" to passing God's tests, this could be it. INCREASE OUR "BELIEVING GOD." That's something unique, isn't it?!? Every preacher has stood in his pulpit and many times has simply said, "Believe God! Believe God! Believe God!"

Every test is all about what we believe about God, not about what we believe about ourselves, our capabilities.

Too many Christians focus on what they believe about themselves, their capabilities. This leads to the "bad feelings" which lead to depression. Depression is the failure of trusting self and losing, versus trusting God and winning (being an overcomer).

There is no test if it is not greater than what we currently are.

In one of the most crucial aspects of a test, we use what faith we ALREADY have when a test comes. We don't GET MORE faith during a test. The very idea that a test must be of something greater than what we have already passed is something we ought to know, but we somehow don't get this and use it. We are tested until we pass, then we are tested on a greater Truth. When we pass, we have grown in His grace and His faith. But, yikes! There will come a greater test! Well, amen.

We are called "rebellious" when we don't pass a test of faith.

This is an ugly truth to swallow. But, it is Truth. Each test is for God's glory, as well as my good. What is not passing a test? Not believing God. What is not believing God? Rebellion against God. How could we miss such a simple Truth? IF we are cognizant and constantly aware of our rebellion, we would perhaps tend to "believe God," if only for the sake of avoiding rebelliousness! After all, we know what God has to say about "rebelliousness," don't we? "Rebellion is as the sin of witchcraft, and stubbornness is as iniquity and idolatry" (1 Samuel 15:23).

To be ready for a test, we must remember never to forget what God has taught us.

Dr. Wilkinson gives us 7 outstanding ways to "practice" and prepare before we face a test. These include reading the Bible daily/ regularly, having a personal journal to record our life with Him (actually, this and all books I am writing in my latter years comprise a compilation of my journals, notes, notations in my bibles, etc.), get into the habit of repeating 10 recent works of God in our life… and give Him thanks, read about and implement what great Saints before have done in their tests of faith, have different "memorials" (something we keep, or build, or record in a unique way…a tangible object) to remind us and that we can draw upon in the future, have some songs that speak of the Lord's faithfulness (especially ones that speak directly to something He did in your life), and finally: tell your family about the tests of your faith and especially how God came through when you were counting on Him.

All our failures of tests are about what we believe about the future. We can't see God coming through for us, or trust that His promises will be fulfilled.

Wow! Here again is an eye-opener! We get so focused on what is going on right NOW, that we miss what God is going to do at a future moment, perhaps the NEXT moment.

This involves our knowing and trusting a promise of God. How often do we think of God's promises? Trying to hang on is looking only at the present. Finding a promise of God is looking to the future. We will endure in any test only if we believe and take hold of God's promises.

Our action in a test is a testimony of what we believe about the character of God.

Don't forget: every test is a lesson about what God says about Himself! What He is like. Who He is. His character. How do you and I feel about the "giver" of each test? How much do we know about His nature? And ultimately, what can we count on Him for…and why? Listen…all of God's wisdom and all of God's promises are based on the character of God. AMEN!

We often become angry at God when WE FAIL a test

(wow!).This is a reality in too many Christians. Read my chapter on Charles Stanley for more about this. But, know this…many have gotten bitter at God, and left church.

The answer for a feeling of "not knowing what to do" in a test is always one thing: ask God for His wisdom

(re: James 1:5)."Lord, I don't know what to do…please tell me." Don't you just LOVE James 1:5?!? "If any of you lack wisdom, let him ask of God, that giveth to all men liberally, and upbraideth not; and it shall be given him." Do we believe that??? We better!!! Tests will come again and again where His wisdom will enable us to pass the test. One thing though, read vs. 6-8, they speak of "doubters" who show their double-soul (w/2 minds). And, don't forget, the source of the answers for all tests is the PERSON giving tests! What a magnificent and omniscient teacher! The purpose of every test is for our good...and every test comes from God.

Well, amen! What's my next test?

Now, listen...and listen closely: When OUR faith is really HIS FAITH that has become OUR faith, there is never a situation that we should fail a test. The test is actually to find out IF HIS FAITH HAS BECOME OUR FAITH. HIS FAITH never fails a test, no matter WHAT the test is!

Oh, by the way, I also told Dr. Wilkinson that I think God ought to require every believer to go through his study. And that should be once a year. It is that good and that important for our life as a Christian to be pleasing to God.

"Lord Jesus, thank You for sending Bruce Wilkinson into my life. I want Your faith to become my faith, so that when I am tested I will always be found faithful to pass each test. Thank You for teaching me what You will be testing me on. May I be found to be a 'good student' who will always pass Your tests."

Oh yes, I pray that God sends Bruce Wilkinson your way at that precise moment you need to hear a word from God! And remember this...Truth will always find a way!

Chapter Eleven

Bill Gothard – "Truth uncompromised"

"All Scripture is given by inspiration of God..."
2 Timothy 3:16

When we were first Born Again back in 1980, Barbara and I heard lots of people at our church (Sagemont Church, Houston, TX) talk about attending some big conference or workshop that "everyone needed to go to." Well, we inquired in the church office and found out that the deadline for registering for that year had passed...we would have to wait until the following year.

That wasn't too unsettling as we were new Christians, and we were trying to find out what just being a church member, as well as being Born Again, was all about. Little did we know that when we finally got to go the next year, we would be attending an event that would shape our lives, and our daughters' lives, for the rest of our life here on earth...and who knows how many others have had their life made more fervent toward the Truth of God because of the *Institute in Basic Life Principles Conference.*

The Bill Gothard Institute in Basic Life Principles is the most comprehensive bible study of behavior and basic issues of being a Christian in this world. Begun in 1964, it was started as an explanation of Mr. Gothard's work with youth, and his trying to share the commands of Christ, and God's working in lives that respond positively to His words.

For years and years...almost 40...the seagulls have been circling around me constantly, keeping my spiritual eyes and spiritual ears and spiritual understanding focused on Truth. I like being FREE! I love God's TRUTH!

I could not begin to enumerate the awesome Truths I gleaned from our attending several of these conferences, and taking many church members along in my pastoral years. I could not begin to enumerate all the Truths from this great gathering of God's Word that I have used in sermons. But, there is one that sticks with me virtually day in and day out...the narrowness of Truth. Any compromise is a deviation from God.

I dislike the word "compromise." I think it could be one of the most ungodly words man has ever come up with. Like "apologize" instead of "ask forgiveness." (By the way, "apologize" does not appear anywhere in the Holy Scriptures…and "compromise" doesn't either!!! Neither are in God's vocabulary!)

Barbara and I first attended a Bill Gothard *Basic Youth Conflicts Conference* (as it was originally called) in June, 1981, at the Sam Houston Coliseum in Houston, Texas. We learned so many Life Truths in 6 short days! I still have the workbook from that conference. (we took several different church groups from Houston and Canyon Lake to his conference. I attended many of his 1-day pastor's conferences. Barbara and I attended one of his Home School conferences – at the University of Tennessee in Knoxville, TN). Bill Gothard's diagram of a straight line for Truth (top of page to bottom), then showing how the devil tries to move us off Truth and how many are willing to compromise just a little, has had as much impact on me and my preaching/teaching/ministering/living as almost any other Truth I have been given by God. He shows that after a "couple" of compromises, we have moved farther away from Truth than where the devil WAS the first time he got us to compromise. We have moved farther than we would have ever "dared" to go at that first compromise. Think about it. How far have you moved from Truth because of several little compromises on the same subject?!?

You know, ALL of God's Truth is "straight and narrow," very concise, very exact. We would never consider handing a bank teller a $10.00 bill, asking for one $5 and five $1's…and accept them giving us one $5, four $1's, three quarters, two dimes, and four pennies. Would we? SO HOW IS IT WE ARE ACCEPTING OF "almost the Truth," or "a half Truth," or "a LIE" altogether?!?

One of the easiest ways to get sidetracked off Truth is this: definitions. Yes, a simple definition of a word. What is the Truth behind the Word of God? God's meanings. Since the original texts were primarily written in Hebrew (O.T.) and Greek (N.T.), knowing the Hebrew and Greek words behind our English words is a big start. Then there are numerous nuances in the different grammar words of those original languages, particularly the Greek. Knowing the truthful meaning of the exact, specific Hebrew and Greek words is necessary. THEN, and only THEN, can we begin to know Truthfully what God is telling us in HIS WORD. The bibles in English are not intended to be MAN's words, but GOD's words. READ ON!

I began to meditate on this, and one thing that came to mind is Evangelist Billy Graham's use of "The Bible says…" Rarely does Graham say, "Paul said…" or "Peter said…" Over and over he says, "The Bible says…" or "God says…" Why? Well, I wish I could have had the privilege to ask him, but I am as certain as I can be without talking directly with Rev. Graham, that it is because he wanted us to know GOD HAS SPOKEN. "All Scripture is given by inspiration of God…" All Scripture is "God-breathed." Could it be that many of the Christians who are willing to compromise on what "Paul has said," would not do so if they were cognizant and knowing they were compromising on GOD's WORDS???

Ever since that meeting in the Garden of Eden with the serpent and Eve, the devil has constantly been challenging God's Words, God's meanings. For one thing, the original languages translated into our English language can lead to us having mistakes and misunderstandings. We all know that many people define English words differently.

It stands to reason that the devil is ALWAYS trying to get God's children to move away from Truth. For one, Truth is Jesus. Two, Truth makes God's children free. Three, Truth is absolute…no wavering, no meandering, no wiggle-room, no room for compromise! Four, once the devil has a Christian "moved" from Truth, the devil has opportunity to cause confusion. God's Word tells us GOD is not the author of confusion. In 1 Corinthians 14:33, God Himself tells us "For God is not the author of confusion, but of peace…" Nothing brings "peace" to the heart of an abandoned Believer like the Truth of God's Word, Jesus Christ Himself.

Think about it. What peace Christ brings to our life.

Anyone who wants to know the Truth of Scripture must find the original languages and the accurate meanings of those words. Those are the words that Scripture was recorded in. Sometimes translations are not accurate because of the difficulty in moving from one language to another. I found that out when preaching in churches in Mexico and Africa while on mission trips. The translator would turn and say, "We don't have a word in our language that can translate what you are saying. Do you have another word you can use?" Well, we have the texts of both the Old Testament and the New Testament in the original languages. So, there is no excuse for not finding out which word is being translated into English, and what the meaning is in the original language. All of this is why I have used extensively for the last 25 years the books of Spiros Zodhiates, the renowned Greek (and Hebrew) language expert to get to Truth in words and verses I preach and teach and counsel with.

It was Bill Gothard, in 1981 at the Sam Houston Coliseum, who dramatically planted the seed of how precise and concise and exact is Truth of the Word of God. And how the enemy of Christians is always trying to get us to deviate from Truth. What is our problem? Did the enemy not question God's Word from the very beginning: "Yea, hath God said…?" (Genesis 3:2). I would venture to say that every problem I had in the pastorate came from someone deviating from Truth, usually to fit one of their personal desires as opposed to God's.

As I mentioned before, the number of Truths, principles, and practical applications of God's Word and the actions and behaviors of people that I learned from Bill Gothard and his ministry are way too many to list or attempt to describe in this short discourse. My recommendation to all is that you find Gothard's materials and learn them for yourself.

Perhaps as a way of "wetting your whistle" to want to pursue that venture, let me list just a few with a brief description:

- "Character First" – an extensive study of character qualities that are based on the character of God. All of these are gifts to every Believer, available to use in everyday life. Extensions of this material surfaced in a ministry called Character Cities, of which I led our church to participate in. In fact, in Flint, Michigan, at the first Character Cities conference, I participated with other invited speakers to share the church's role in this endeavor. *The Power for True Success: How to Build Character in Your Life* was a book for use in the religious section of this movement. *Achieving True Success: How to Build Character as a Family* was a book for use in schools, businesses, and those governmental entities that participated. The same 49 character qualities were in both books. The first had Scriptures that explained each quality.

- Numerous booklets giving detailed explanations and applications on various aspects of the interaction of man with man, man with God, or man with himself.

Honor Your Parents

How to Turn Family Conflicts Into Blessings

How the "Heart" Determines Direction in Life

Discerning God's Will in Every Decision
Discerning a Spirit of Anger

How to Tear Down the Strongholds of Bitterness

How to Gain a Good Conscience

Lay Up Treasures: The Power of Giving

Bring In the Poor: The Power of Hospitality

Training Up Faithful Men

Training Up Faithful Women

The Commands of Christ

There are powerful teachings in each of these booklets. These along with the extensive instruction in the Basic Seminar are a part of the voluminous information available to glean from scriptures throughout the Bible, the heart-felt teaching of God for His children.

I am grateful to God for the foundational Truths that He gave me through Bill Gothard and the *Institute in Basic Life Principles* ministry. These Truths WILL impact your life!

"Lord Jesus, thank You for bringing Bill Gothard into my life. Virtually all of his teachings gave me multitudes of principles and Truths straight from Your Word, and the experiences You led him through in Youth Ministry and otherwise. Thank You for Your Truth. May you forever keep the hearts of Your Saints mindful, alert, and faithful toward standing firm and not compromising on You and Your Truth. Help us, O Lord, in our unfaithfulness."

Oh yes, I pray that God sends a Bill Gothard your way at that precise moment you need to stand on Truth from God! And remember this... Truth will always find a way!

Chapter Twelve

John Morgan – "When your outgo exceeds your income…"

"But my God shall supply all your need according to His
riches in glory by Christ Jesus."
Philippians 4:19

When it comes to "life verses" and biblical Truths that have been given me which have changed my life forever, John Morgan was my first and one of my most prolific teachers. One thing I learned early on after becoming a Born Again Believer is this: it may take 18+ years from our physical birth for an individual to become mature physically, somewhat fully developed, but it can take just a couple of years for a Christian to "grow a whole lot spiritually" after being Born Again. Growth spiritually comes from exposure to biblical Truth, and believing it. Believing Truth can change someone immediately. And it is possible to believe a lot in a short period of time.

Other than that moment in May, 1980 and Pastor Morgan's message from the Gospel of John, chapter 3, (see chapter 2 of this book), nothing changed our lives more dramatically early on than John Morgan's *Financial Freedom Seminar*. Prior to Barbara and me becoming Christians in 1980 we had been given and taught so many financial things that turned out to be *worldly advice* and *so-called wisdom* that we found out to be false compared to God's Word. It was within just a few weeks after we became involved at Sagemont Church that Barbara came home one evening and told me about some things John Morgan had taught in a Church Training financial class at church that Sunday evening (Church Training classes— that's a novel thought that disappeared from most Bible churches years ago). Pastor Morgan had compiled his Financial Freedom course at the church the year before, then led the people to get out of debt individually and at the same time give over $1,000,000 in 40 DAYS to get the church out of debt…this was in 1979! Testimonies abounded of *miracles* happening when the people began to trust God, and the Word of God, and to give to God as He has instructed in His Word.

This was completely foreign teaching to me.

Everything I had learned from the world regarding finances focused around debt and leveraging money, an investment strategy of using borrowed money to generate large investment returns. We had a friend who was a banker that told of buying a house on as little down as possible, then selling in a year or two, then taking the capital gain and reinvesting that in a larger, more expensive home. He had repeated this process three or four times that netted him a huge home with about the same payment as the first one, with no additional cash investment out of his pockets save the capital gains. His teaching was always based on: "don't use your own money…use someone else's."

Let me quickly add: it may be possible to do as this man did, when markets are stable and rising, and never have a downfall. But even with that, if a process is not God's way, it is the wrong way for Christians. Do you remember the fellow in Luke chapter 12, verses 13-21?

> "And one of the company said unto Him, 'Master, speak to my brother, that he divide the inheritance with me.' And He said unto him, 'Man, who made Me a judge or a divider over you?' And He said unto them, 'Take heed, and beware of covetousness: for a man's life consisteth not in the abundance of the things which he possesseth.' And He spake a parable unto them, saying, 'The ground of a certain rich man brought forth plentifully: And he thought within himself, saying, What shall I do, because I have no room where to bestow all my fruits and my goods. And I will say to my soul, Soul, thou hast much goods laid up for many years; take thine ease, eat, drink, and be merry'. But God said unto him, 'Thou fool, this night thy soul shall be required of thee: then whose shall those things be, which thou hast provided?' So is he that layeth up treasure for himself, and is not rich toward God."

Or, what Paul told Timothy in 1 Timothy 6:6-12?

> "But godliness with contentment is great gain. For we brought nothing into this world, and it is certain we can carry nothing out. And having food and raiment, let us be therewith content. But they that will be rich fall into temptation and a snare, and into many foolish and hurtful lusts, which drown men in destruction and perdition. For the love of money is the root of all evil: which while some coveted after, they have erred from

the faith, and pierced themselves through with many sorrows. But thou, O man of God, flee these things, and follow after righteousness, godliness, faith, love, patience, meekness. Fight the good fight of faith, lay hold on eternal life, whereunto thou are also called, and hast professed a good profession before many witnesses."

I believe the introduction of wide-spread, "low-cost" borrowing of funds in the early 1950's began what is now the financial instability and ultimate ruin of the American economic structure. When a people (nation of people) do not do things God's way, the ruin of their way of life is inevitable. Some day, one day, America's financial world will crumble due to the ungodly path our leaders have taken us. Even today we are seeing unfold before our very eyes what God told His people back in Deut. 28:12, 15:

(v.12) "The LORD shall open unto thee His good treasure, the heaven to give the rain unto thy land in His season, and to bless all the work of thine hand: and thou shalt lend unto many nations, and thou shalt not borrow."

(v.15) "But it shall come to pass, if thou wilt not hearken unto the voice of the LORD thy God, to observe to do all His commandments and His statutes which I command thee this day; that all these curses shall come upon thee, and overtake thee"

(vs. 16-19 list horrible things that happen when God's people do not hearken unto His voice).

But, the main things I want to focus on in this section are four (4) great biblical Truths that John Morgan pointed out and shared with us. I am not enumerating these in any particular order of importance. Each has been a "Life Truth" that has dictated to Barbara and me decisions we have made with our own personal finances.

1. **"When your outgo exceeds your income, your upkeep becomes your downfall."** John Morgan taught us this. This is certainly one of the first Truths that we began to consider. And this is a SEAGULL Truth if there ever was one. Anytime our outgo exceeds our income there is only one way to continue…BORROW to pay for the amount spent over our income. Borrowing is going into debt. And God says that debt is never to be incurred by His people.

"…thou shalt lend unto many nations, and thou shalt not borrow."

Deut. 28:12 again

Debt is easy to incur. It may have been easier in the 80's and 90's than today, but it is easy to incur. Credit card debt is the easiest. The problem for most people is that they have no clue as to the total amount of actual money they owe when they are addicted to credit card spending. Who actually keeps track of every transaction? Or, the total of the transactions made since the last payment to the credit card company? Or, the total amount owed to the credit card company?

For over 35 years I have taught the scriptures, Truths, and principles I learned from John Morgan's *Financial Freedom Seminar*. I have been what I call a Financial Coach for as long as I have been in ministry. I have said that I could get anyone out of debt in one year or less (it requires some difficult decisions and actions that many do not want to take, but it is always possible).

The one thing that has always surfaced when trying to determine one's total outgo is that folks have no written down record of such, and they cannot remember every payment they make each month! Incredible! Yet, again and again, the 2nd, 3rd, and sometimes 4th follow-up visit yielded an "Oh, we forgot we pay ??? about $xx a month…it's not much, we just didn't remember that." In every case of Coaching, the people's OUTGO EXCEEDED THEIR INCOME. They were getting further in debt simply by this practice, not to mention their outgo included MINIMUM payments for DEBT OWED to several institutions.

John Morgan taught us to do a MONTHLY INCOME/OUTGO statement. We STILL do this today…to the PENNY! We like to call it: operating as "Mr. & Mrs. Lee McDowell, un-incorporated." Financial records, financial tracking, and knowing your financial cash flow are as important as anything one can do. (I can't tell you all the different emotions that surfaced in me during my tenure as a Pastor for over 30 years from the almost 100% of church members who would not dare consider the church having NO financial records/budget/monthly meetings with financial accountability…yet they have NO such financial dealings in their own home! That's insane, isn't it?!? not to mention, ungodly.)

Not spending more than God has provided is a biblical Truth. Nowhere in the Bible do we find God telling His people to borrow to spend. In fact, John Morgan taught us a great Truth about God's

99

provision and spending: it is what the Apostle Paul said in Philippians chapter 4, verse 19:

> "But my God shall supply all your need according to His riches in glory by Christ Jesus."

"All your need." So why would any Christian feel it necessary, or even possibly consider it Christ-honoring, to borrow money at any time? We either trust God to supply all we need, or we don't.

2. **"Make decisions that will make other decisions for you."** John Morgan taught us this. This is not a 2+2=4 truth, but it has dramatic impact on anyone's financial picture. SEAGULLS do this. You will never find them circling and diving for trash fish, etc. That's what terns, the *liar birds*, do. Seagulls only go after shrimp that speckled trout or redfish are chasing to the top of the water. Seagulls have decided they only want shrimp, not trash. They have decided this ahead of time...ahead of ever seeing shrimp or trash!

Against everything and every way that we had learned from the world, Barbara and I got out of debt in 1981. And we have lived "debt-free" since then. Pastor John Morgan taught us in his *Financial Freedom Seminar* that borrowing money (at any time, from anybody) is against what the Bible teaches. And being debt-free is FREEDOM! And doing so is a huge Life-decision. For instance, once you have decided to get out of debt, not incur any more debt, and then Live as we like to call it: "Trust God for His supply, and Live on it," you have made three decisions that will make many other decisions for you. These are simple Truths, but very relevant to Living a comfortable, uncomplicated, and predictable Life. And Life like that is good and peaceful, and complete freedom. This became a conviction, not a preference.

For us, that leads to having a Spending Plan (we prefer that over the term *budget*) that really guides us in making financial decisions for a month at a time. That leads to NOT making some *off-the-wall* decision that can throw our finances into a stressful situation. Paying cash for everything, including cars, is as stress-less as Life can be. NOT HAVING ANY MONTHLY PAYMENT OBLIGATIONS FOR EXPENSES INCURRED PRIOR TO THE START OF EVERY MONTH is a stress-free way of Life. In fact, I recommend that you get yourself into a position of having enough money in your checking account on the first day of each month that will cover your entire month's outgo. How would you like to have that situation each and every month?!? What about unexpected emergency expenditures, replacing autos or major appliances, or vacations??? Cover those with one or more savings accounts, designed to PLAN ahead for such situations…with deposits to those savings accounts figured into your Regular Monthly Spending Plan! (I am in the process of compiling materials for another book: *The Math of Life*. In it I will discuss my "15-15-25-45 Plan" for figuring a monthly spending plan.)

John Morgan taught us all this. These have proven to be the most freedom-giving, joy-bringing, peace-providing Truths that we have contentsenjoyed since 1981…in many, many different areas of our lives.

Matthew 6:21 and Luke 12:34 tell us:

"For where your treasure is, there will be your heart also."

What a powerful proclamation of the link between our treasure and our heart. I remember John Morgan always speaking of biblical finances being a matter showing where our heart is. It is either with God, or against Him.

P.S. Here is something that has nothing to do with finances, but is another way this Truth can work for you. Years ago, Barbara and I made one of the greatest decisions we have ever made, and it was because of this simple truth (#2) that John Morgan taught us. It was this: "I cannot NOT forgive." It became a conviction for us, not a preference. No matter WHAT anyone has said or done to us, we forgive them in Christ. The flesh may not want to forgive, but our Spirit and Christ's Soul in us do. We must. And as Philippians 4:13 says, "I can do ALL things through Christ Who strengthens me." It is really Him, and not us. Well, amen!

3. **"The borrower is servant to the lender."** John Morgan taught us this. God taught him that in Proverbs 22:7, "The rich ruleth over the poor, and the borrower is servant to the lender."

John Morgan taught us that we might lend (or, better, he said: "give"), but that we should never borrow. God has said again and again He will supply our need.

> "The LORD shall open unto thee His good treasure, the heaven to give the rain unto thy land in His season, and to bless all the work of thine hand: and thou shalt lend unto many nations, and shalt not borrow." Deuteronomy 28:12

John Morgan taught us that becoming surety for a family member, a friend, or a stranger is prohibited:

> "My son, if thou be surety for thy friend, if thou hast stricken thy hand with a stranger, thou art snared with the words of thy mouth, thou art taken with the words

of thy mouth. Do this now, my son, and deliver thyself,
when thou art come into the hand of thy friend; go,
humble thyself, and make sure thy friend." Proverbs 6:1

These don't need any explanation, do they? They are self-explanatory. DO NOT BORROW. The borrower is servant to the lender. And further, God has told us we are to serve only One...Him.

"No servant can serve two masters: for either he will
hate the one, and love the other; or else he will hold to
the one, and despise the other. Ye cannot serve God and
mammon. And the Pharisees also, who were covetous,
heard all these things: and they derided Him. And He
said unto them, Ye are they which justify yourselves
before men; but God knoweth your hearts: for that
which is highly esteemed among men is abomination in
the sight of God." Luke 16:13-15

I can still hear Pastor Morgan say: "God says He will supply all we need. The devil likes to whisper in our ear and say, 'If your God won't give it to you right now, sign here (borrow/credit) and you can have it now.'"

John Morgan showed us God's Truth about borrowing, and we will NOT borrow money for anything. (p.s. having trouble finding or knowing God's will/way for whether you should purchase something...especially a car or a boat, etc.? HAS GOD already supplied the money for you to purchase whatever it is??? The answer to this last question is this: YES. God has ALWAYS ALREADY supplied the cash to make ANY purchase BEFORE you are to purchase anything!)

4. **"You cannot outgive God."** John Morgan taught us this. God taught him that in the following scriptures:

"Honor the LORD with thy substance, and with the
firstfruits of all thine increase: So shall thy barns be filled
with plenty, and thy presses shall burst out with new
wine." Proverbs 3:9-10

(notice God says Give from what we already have – substance –
AND Give from off-the-top - firstfruits - of all He brings our way.)

"Will a man rob God? Yet ye have robbed Me. But ye
say, Wherein have we robbed Thee? In tithes and
offerings. Ye are cursed with a curse: for ye have robbed
Me, even this whole nation. Bring ye all the tithes into
the storehouse, that there may be meat in Mine house,
and prove Me now herewith, saith the LORD of hosts,

102

if I will not open you the windows of heaven, and pour out a blessing, that there shall not be room enough to receive it. And I will rebuke the devourer for your sakes, and he shall not destroy the fruits of your ground; neither shall your vine cast her fruit before the time in the field, saith the LORD of hosts. And all nations shall call you blessed: for ye shall be a delightful land, saith the LORD of hosts." Malachi 3:8-12

"Give, and it shall be given unto you; good measure, pressed down, and shaken together, and running over, shall men give unto your bosom. For with the same measure that ye mete withal it shall be measured to you again." Luke 6:38

(look at EVERY word and examine how God gives us more than we give!)

Well, it was no surprise to hear Pastor Morgan speak so overwhelmingly in favor of having hearts that were giving-oriented. We came to Sagemont Church one year after he led the people in 1979 to give - in addition to their regular tithes and missions giving - all the money God brought each family's way for a 40 day period...in order to get the church completely out of debt. There were 300 families that committed and went through a six-month preparation period (getting out of debt, figuring how much it would take to live for 40 days, saving up the amount they had calculated they would need, figuring ways to reduce expenses during the "40 Days," and making themselves available for God to bring in additional money besides their regular paychecks). One of the most incredible ways the people managed to live on less for those 40 days was through the "soup kitchen" at the church many nights where cornbread, beans, or soup was provided for the families to save lots of money on supper costs.

God opened the windows of heaven and showered many of these families with much more than their "regular income." The amounts were more than the people could have imagined was possible. That "income" was really "debt retirement gifts." The people have told of happenings that are nothing less than what can be explained as simply "God." One family thought they would be unable to give, but signed up anyway to participate...received an inheritance, and they gave ALL of the amount. Many gave offerings above their paychecks. The total of offerings to the "40 Days Offering" was a little in excess of $1,000,000! God provided a group of people with willing hearts, giving hearts, to get their church out of debt at a time when interest rates were "choking" some businesses and some individuals (and many churches!) severely.

A phenomenal story at the start of this endeavor was a need that came to the pastor's attention of a family in the neighborhood whose wife/mother had cancer and couldn't afford medical treatment. Sagemont Church voted to GIVE that family $40,000 from their "40 Days Fund." Try telling the folks at Sagemont Church back then that it is possible to "out give God."

I did learn an eye-opening lesson from that banker I mentioned earlier: "pay yourself first." It was a great lesson at the time, around 1975. Up until then I had been told and believed that it was perfectly fine, actually "brilliant," to live like there is no tomorrow. To live and operate on someone else's money…"don't use your own money"…was a way of life for us. So, we saw nothing wrong with borrowing to buy cars, etc. Borrowing to go on vacations. Borrowing even to go out to eat (charge it). Borrow, borrow, borrow. But then our banker friend told me a *secret* of his: *pay yourself first.* This needs a little explaining. Our banker used the following illustration:

> "The world advertises, 'You deserve a break today.' Translated, that means 'Go out on the town and celebrate your income. You've earned it.' But in the morning, who ends up with your money? The world has. And you usually don't have anything to put away in savings after all the celebrating. To get ahead, you must 'pay yourself first.' Put something into your savings, then maybe go celebrate."

But just a few years later when we came to know the Lord Jesus Christ as our Savior and were Born Again, our thinking and "wanting" changed. Why? Because God had given us a new "wanter" (remember what Pastor Morgan had told Barbara and me in his office right after we had prayed to trust Christ as our Savior? – chapter 2). And we wanted whatever God says. And God said things that contradicted the world's way of economic decisions and activity. SO…we revised our economic priorities and the banker's teaching to reflect God's teaching:

- We always give to God first, what He has said we should give.
- Next then, *we pay ourself.* We decided IN our Spending Plan that once we had given to God what He asked for, THEN we would *pay ourself* what our economic plan told us we needed to save for all "future" needs, setting aside for upcoming expenses that are incurred once or twice a year (repairs/maintenance, insurance, taxes, etc.

- Finally, we *live on the rest*. That includes food, clothing, household expenses (electricity, water, etc.), eating out and any other entertainment, auto gas & oil and all of the ways in which money seems to "disappear."
- We do not spend one dollar more than our Monthly Financial Plan.
- (you may ask: "How do you pay for *large* or *unexpected* items/expenses?" Our Monthly Financial Plan includes the Savings of *pay ourselves first* which includes an auto fund, vacation fund, appliance fund, etc., etc.)

When we give to God first, and give to God His ways He has taught us, He always gives back to us in measure as we have given to Him… plus some!

> "Give and it shall be given unto you; good measure, pressed down, and shaken together, and running over, shall men give into your bosom. For with the same measure that ye mete withal it shall be measured to you again." Luke 6:38

For 38 years it has been enough to cover whatever God gives us direction to give, to do, or to purchase. Well, amen!

Now, I have to admit. We don't see many seagulls flying overhead in the piney woods of East Texas. BUT, we know they are there somewhere!

Because, as you can see, the Truth that John Morgan brought to our life created a dramatic change from the way we had been taught and had done things for years. But the great thing is that for these last 38 years we have lived "financially free." The Truth always MAKES you FREE!

"Lord Jesus, thank You once more for bringing John Morgan into my life and Barbara's. Thank You for leading me (and Barbara) to always trust only in Your provision, and to live on what You have provided for us. We are grateful we GET to Live the Abundant Life of Christ in our daily finances.

Oh, yes…once again, I hope and pray God sends a John Morgan into your life at just the right moment! And remember this…Truth will always find a way!

Chapter Thirteen

Bill Sevier – "We show up, God gives the increase"

"He that is faithful in that which is least is faithful also in
much: and he that is unjust in the least is unjust also in much."
Luke 16:10

Bill Sevier taught me how to visit, witness, and help people to trust Jesus Christ as their Savior. Not bad for a NASA engineer.

On the first day Barbara and I visited Sagemont Baptist Church, of all things we ended up going to Sunday School right after the church service. Hey, it was crazy we were visiting a Baptist Church for the church service to start with, but Sunday School? Don't ask me for a reason "why" we did that. We just followed the flow of going to get the gift of a Family Bible given to visitors right after the close of the church service, and the next thing I know we are upstairs in a room full of folks our age, some of whom Barbara knew. There was one fellow, Rick Jones, I had known from my boat business days. He invited me to sit by him for the announcements, etc. And moments later, Bill Sevier (who was the YA2L Sunday School department director) is scaring me half to death because he called on Rick to pray, leading me to think the whole time of the prayer that if I came back next week Bill would call on me! (Don't ask me How or Why!).

Well, as you know, Barbara and I were Born Again in Pastor Morgan's office 2 days later, and things and people began to change rapidly in our lives. Two of those folks we became dramatically involved with were Bill and Maxine Sevier. Turns out, they lived just down the street and around one corner. And 3 months later, Bill is asking us to pray about moving to another SS department he and Maxine were going to lead in the new Sunday School year. He wanted me to be the Outreach Leader for the department!

Part of the responsibilities of the Department Outreach Leader was to keep track of prospects for the department, which included folks who had just visited the church. The SS Office would let us know when a new visitor had been to church.

Now, remember, this is long before computers and printed lists, or hand-held smart phones with all the info at our fingertips wherever we are. Did you know that Baptists used to "play cards" way back then on Wednesday nights?!? That's right! (Oh, what a "nasty habit"). I had found out in the three months we had been "saved" (lingo for "Born Again" that didn't seem so offensive to some church folks) that Baptists didn't dance! No more Gilley's for Barbara and me. Anyhow, Bill took me to the eastern wall of that gymnatorium the first Wednesday night after the start of the new Sunday School year. Over against the wall of the gym (remember, it was the "auditorium" or "sanctuary" on Sunday mornings and nights, but on Wednesday nights it was the Family Meal place at 5pm, bible study place at 6:30pm, and where the "card tables" were the center of attention at 7:30pm), all lined up were those dark brown, 8' long, folding tables ALL FULL OF CARDS. These weren't the ordinary canasta or gin cards in people's homes. These were cards with "prospects" names and addresses on them. Anyhow, each Wednesday night, the folks would go where the placards on some tall dowel rods indicated the different age groups for the SS Depts. Bill and I went to the "YA1" pole. That was for the adults of one of the youngest age group divisions. We would sort through the cards, like looking for the *ace in the hole* card that would give us the best visit!

> Something I have seen happen in the last few years. The enemy has come along and taken away that "nasty habit" of playing cards (or, using whatever method of sharing the names and contact info of visitors to the church services is available today) along with individuals who are committed and faithful to visit, contact, and follow-up with church visitors. Today there is virtually NO OUTREACH and NO PERSONAL WITNESSING and NO CONCERN for the lost and the unchurched. I don't understand it. If it hadn't been for so many of the various types of contacts from Sagemont Church, I cannot imagine we would have ever visited there on May 18, 1980.

I learned something very important on one of the first Wednesday nights we went visiting. Bill turned to me as we were *shuffling* the cards and said this, "Lee, I've learned long ago that if we are just faithful to go knock on some doors, God will be faithful to bring new folks to visit… even if we don't find anyone at home tonight – or, the ones we visit don't ever come back." I have never forgotten those words. I have witnessed many "seagull" moments over the years where real life proved this Truth!

Numerous times we would leave the church with our chosen cards in our pockets, stop before we drove out of the parking lot to pray for whomever we might go to see, find our way with that Key Map "book of maps" of local streets (Barbara and I still have one! are they worth anything???). Bill didn't know that since I was 5 years old my mother wouldn't leave home in our new place to live without taking me with her. I have some sort of honing device in my brain. Well, when we got to the house address we would find no one at home. Funny thing: Bill never got discouraged. Remember, he said, "If we are faithful to knock on some doors…"

Let me stop a minute and ask you something: are you "faithful" at the things God has given you to do? Has God found you "faithful" in the "little things"? It is incredibly important to notice one small 2-letter word in the midst of Luke 16:10: "is." There has been a lot of discussion over the years as to what "is" is, but let us rest assured God has no trouble with that word. God says, "He that **IS faithful** in that which **IS** least **IS faithful** also in **much**: and he that **IS unjust** in the **least IS** unjust also in **much**." Bill Sevier taught me a huge lesson on those Wednesday nights.

I have to tell you of a couple of the best nights. Really soon after being in this Outreach Leader position, Bill and I go to visit a young couple who had visited the church the Sunday before. When we rang the doorbell, the man answered and here he is standing in the finest southern cowboy gear you can imagine. His wife peaked in for a moment, with a sure-fire square-dancing flare skirt on. Yep. They were headed to a square-dance class to learn those moves I could never begin to remember. Anyhow, for no more than five minutes we found out they had visited because the wife's aunt had passed away recently, and they had begun to "think about God." Having two young kids made a difference in all that also (reminiscent of Barbara and me). And, we quickly said, "We will get back with you soon, and hope to see you this next Sunday at SS." Well, to make a long story short, they came back to Sagemont Baptist, became a part of our SS Dept, and soon thereafter the wife was Born Again and baptized. The husband? He was thinking about it.

A couple of months later, the husband called me. He wanted to meet with Bill and me to discuss this matter further. Bill and I joined the husband at his kitchen table on a Saturday morning later that week, and he prayed to trust Jesus Christ as his Savior right there. Beautiful!

One other time, Bill and I headed out to see a fellow whose wife was coming to our church, even singing in the choir. He was at home with their child and at least one pet. I learned another "faithful" lesson that night! Bill Sevier was a man of many years of visiting experience. He knew that the enemy would use whatever he could to distract and derail any presentation of the Gospel. So, I was assigned in these first visits to put the dog in the garage and get something to read or play with the kids in one corner of the living room while Bill launched into his routine Gospel presentation. Perhaps he didn't know, but I always had an ear to what he was saying to the ones whose attention he had. Well, quite a few hectic moments later (for me, at least!), Bill says, "Bro. Lee, let me introduce you to a new brother in Christ!" Yep, faithful in the least (or, little things) will yield results just like being faithful in much (bigger things).

Bill Sevier worked down in Clear Lake with the astronauts in the Space Center. His expertise was with their space suits. Faithfulness in being careful with small details that could be absolutely critical to the safety of the astronauts was in his blood…his engineering blood. Bill's expertise at the church was faithfulness to know every one of the people in his department, faithfulness to make contacts on Saturday nights to those who might have missed a Sunday or two, faithfulness to pray for those on our prayer list, faithfulness to take the time to lead and train and encourage his co-workers, faithfulness to go the 2nd mile and knock on hundreds of doors seeking to share God's love and Christ's Gospel of Good News of salvation. And he taught me and exhorted me to much of his faithfulness.

Here I am at 73 years of age. Going to a local park here in Nacogdoches, TX, each Sunday morning with some coffee and snacks, and just "showing up." Not long ago, on a cold, wet morning, one of the "new" guys who joined us in "Christ In The Park" said to me: "I didn't think you would make it this morning." I simply said, "I am committed to just show up each Sunday morning and see who is interested in hearing about Jesus." Many Sundays, there must be some seagulls flying around. Truth finds its way into someone wandering through the park, when they stop to drink coffee, eat a bit, and hear ordinary people talking about Jesus Christ.

> God has a wonderful way of sending seagulls to mysterious places. The idea for this park ministry came from a guy (Greg Wray) who owns an auto repair shop in California, at a Michael Wells' Men's Retreat in Colorado, almost 20 years ago! Greg and I met and were staying in a cabin with a few other guys at this large retreat center. One time while we were getting acquainted, Greg tells me of a "house church" he was a part of, and one of

the other participants had this "park ministry"... I thought at the time, what a neat idea. I hoped God would give me opportunity to do something like that one day...

You know, I have used this Truth in so many different ways in my life. I have encouraged so many others to listen to God, and give Him an opportunity to prove His Word to them. How about you? Are you ready to take all the Truths presented to you in this book...testimonies of some of God's finest servants...and begin to apply Truth to your life?

"Lord Jesus, thank You for bringing Bill Sevier into my life. I, too, want to be found a 'faithful' servant. Help me to always have a heart to be abandoned to You in such a way that Your faithfulness lives out in my life. Faithfulness in sharing the Good News of Jesus Christ is so important. Bring a revival and renewal of this sharing to my life today!"

Oh, yes...I hope and pray God sends a Bill Sevier into your life at just the right moment! And remember this...Truth will always find a way!

Chapter Fourteen

Travis B. Bryan, Jr. – "I Hate To Lose"

"I have fought a good fight, I have finished
my course, I have kept the faith."
2 Timothy 4:7

For the life of me, I cannot remember the date I first met Travis B. Bryan, Jr. But I do remember it was the first time we played golf at what was then called the Bryan Municipal Golf Course. Someone on the golf team had told me about this man who had played on the Texas A&M golf team around 1950. Here it was the spring of 1964 and we were getting ready to tee it up for the first time.

I was with a couple of Texas A&M golf team members as we drove up into the gravel parking lot, and parked right next to a fellow getting his clubs out of his trunk and putting on his golf shoes. I was introduced to Mr. Bryan. The first thing out of his mouth was "Lee McDowell (in a tone and manner as ONLY Travis B. Bryan, Jr. could say it!), I'm gonna clip you today!" All the while he was moving his fingers on his right hand in a scissor-like "clipping" manner. In all the years I was privileged to tee it up with Mr. Bryan, he would greet me with those same words, and same motion! Lord, have mercy. We fought like two pit bulls who were striving to stake a claim to one's territory!

Now, keep in mind, Mr. Bryan was President of 1st National Bank of Bryan, and a very honorable man around town, both in the city of Bryan (named after one of his forefathers) and College Station (5 miles south and the home of Texas A&M University). Except when he got on a golf course…he became a serious competitor.

God gifted me with a great friend, great encourager, and great Christian example back then. All the guys knew Mr. Bryan was a Believer. All the guys knew Mr. Bryan was a testimony to His Lord. I got to know Travis (he let me call him that the last couple of years I was at A&M, when no one was around to hear!) as a mentor and supporter. We all had great admiration and respect for Mr. Bryan.

The guys used to call him "Trav" when he wasn't within earshot. And we looked forward to competing and being with Trav. And we all knew he hated to lose!

Anyone who has played any sport, especially in a competitive manner (amateur or professional), knows that the heart of the game is winning. As one fire-ball preacher once proclaimed, "Show me a good loser, and I will show you a Loser." Mr. Bryan was a winner, and he gave me the finest understanding of 2 Timothy 4:7 of any Saint I know. I could fill an entire book with stories from golf outings, to clubhouse banter, to coffee at 1ˢᵗ National Bank about Life from a man who walked with Jesus every day.

I will be the first to admit, I love to compete. Still do at age 73. I don't play golf any more, but put me in the water with a fishing pole and bait and I will want to catch more fish AND the biggest fish of anyone I am fishing with that day! Put me into a game of Yahtzee, Clue, or Catan with the kids and grandkids, and I don't like losing. (LOL! Neither do they!). There is something about "hating to lose" that is very Christian!

The Apostle Paul was that way. Listen to one of the greatest battles he fought, and lost: (for sake of space I will have to ask you to read Acts chapter 26 in its entirety yourself, but listen to the last six verses...)

> "King Agrippa, believest thou the prophets? I know that thou believest. Then Agrippa said unto Paul,
> **Almost thou persuadest me to be a Christian. And Paul said, I would to God, that not only thou, but also all that hear me this day, were both almost, and altogether such as I am, except these bonds.** And when he had thus spoken, the king rose up, and the governor, and Bernice, and they that sat with them: And when they were gone aside, they talked between themselves, saying, This man doeth nothing worthy of death or of bonds. Then said Agrippa unto Festus, This man might have been set at liberty, if he had not appealed unto Caesar." Acts 26:27-32

Paul had fought with many, witnessed to all, and hated to lose any soul from coming to Christ. Mr. Bryan hated to lose any *battle* he entered into. It is Christian to hate to lose.

Another time the Apostle Paul put it this way...

"But we have this treasure in earthen vessels, that the excellency of the power may be of God, and not of us.

We are troubled on every side, yet not distressed; we are perplexed, but not in despair; persecuted, but not forsaken; cast down, but not destroyed; always bearing about in the body the dying of the Lord Jesus, that the life also of Jesus might be made manifest in our body."
2 Corinthians 4:7-10

Paul knew what going into battle was like. Paul knew that being a Loser would be to be a quitter, never winning. Paul was a competitor. Mr. Bryan was every bit the competitor that the Apostle Paul was.

One last scriptural aspect for you. The Apostle John, "the Disciple Jesus loved," gave us the picture of a *winner*. Actually, it silently speaks of "hating to lose," while yielding to that "power that worketh in us" (Ephesians 3:20):

"For whatsoever is born of God, **overcometh** the world: and this is the **victory** that **overcometh** the world, even our faith. Who is he that **overcometh** the world, but he that believeth that Jesus is the Son of God?" 1 John 5:4-5

Overcomers. Victory. Overcometh the world. How? The Bible says "our faith," but God has told us He is the Author of "our faith." It is His Faith that becomes "our faith" when we *really* believe Him and His Word.

All our favorite Saints in all of Scripture were winners, and winners "hate to lose." Travis B. Bryan, Jr. was a winner who really "hated to lose." Travis B. Bryan, Jr. gave me a first-hand experience of seeing, engaging, and learning from a genuine Saint that losing is not for Christians.

On Friday night, May 11, 2008, several golf team members from the 1950's, 1960's, and 1970's gathered at one of the old restaurants in Bryan for memory's sake: the Travis B. Bryan, Jr's TAMU golf reunion. Travis and his wife, Norma, were there. Their sons, Travis B. Bryan III, and Tim Bryan, were there. Joe and Marcia Oden were there. Some of the biggest names in Aggie golf were able to be present that night. Billy Martindale, Jimmy Fetters, Dickie Duble, John Lively, Jr., Mike Higgins, Eugene Bird, Ralph Johnston, Wayne Stroman, Jeff Andrick, David Holcomb, Ray "Chi Chi" Neal, John Buffin, Duke Butler, Richard Ellis, Steve Veriato, Wayne Batten, Perry Arthur, James R. Toland, Doug Dyer, W. A. "Buck"

Prewitt, Billy Wade, Skip Bresk, Jr., Terry Archer, Tommy Shelton, Larry Gorzycki, David Rhodes, Homer Callaway, and Leslie Clifton joined Bully Batten (who put the whole weekend together) and me to honor Mr. Bryan. One great notable who was unable to attend was Bobby Nichols, who was playing in a PGA event at Firestone CC. Also, Al Jones, who was in a friend's wedding in Germany. This gathering was a tribute to the man of God that taught us more than just about winning or losing.

The next morning, May 12th, we gathered for a breakfast at Briarcrest CC, Travis Bryan's home course. Gifts and gab were the menu of the morning with the food just being an aside. There were some who ventured out onto the golf course afterwards. One of the highlights of the morning for me was the daughter and son-in-law of our former coach, Henry Ransom. What a special delight it was to visit with Joe and Marcia Oden about her father, Coach Ransom, and Travis Bryan, and the fellowship of those two great men who had impacted our lives. The two events were a delightful time of reuniting former golf team members, and to spend time in the presence of Mr. Bryan.

I love the story of my teammate, Jeff Andrick (who has been one of the finest Christian business men and friends I have known since the 60's), recounting one conversation with Mr. Bryan, "One time Travis said to me, 23-11-6. I said what in the world does that mean? He said I've beat you 23, you beat me 11 and we've tied 6. I said, are you documenting every time we play?" But, listen to Jeff telling about a visit to 1st National Bank to get Mr. Bryan's autograph on the cap Jeff got that night of the golf reunion. Picture with me Jeff and Trav speaking... "When I went up to his office and got him to sign the cap he was sitting at Gladys' desk in the hall. As I was leaving, when I got to the elevator, he said, 'Jeffaria.' I said 'What'? He said, 'I love you.' I said 'I love you too, Travis.' That may have been the last time I saw him."

That, my friends, is what r-e-s-p-e-c-t is all about.

Since Mr. Bryan is not around to deny me the opportunity, I would like to share one time I "clipped him." Right after Barbara and I were married, we went to San Antonio, TX, for me to play in the 1967 Texas Amateur Golf Championship at the Pecan Valley Golf Course. Play started on Tuesday. 72 holes later on Friday afternoon, I had won the tournament with Mr. Bryan looking on. Even though I signaled to him that he had been clipped that day, he got the last "win." He took the huge trophy the winner gets to keep for a year back to Bryan and displayed it in the 1st National Bank for 12 months. Since I was not around in the bank that much, I cannot know if he ever told anyone of the many times he had "clipped" the Champion on the Bryan Muny!

For all of us, we were saddened to hear of Travis' death. However, he was moving on into the very eternal presence of our Lord Jesus Christ. I was able to be at his homegoing service at the First Baptist Church of Bryan on September 28, 2009. One of Travis' sons, Tim, spoke of how impressive the makeup of the gathering was: "not just the 'high and the mighty' but an equal number of blue collar folks as well as Hispanics and Blacks...the very old on down to the 20 somethings. And they all had a story about their personal relationship with 'Travis' or 'Mr. Bryan.' He had a lot of people that were proud of their friendship with him."

It was special to be sitting among the former Texas A&M golfers who spent so much time with him on the links. It was special hearing the testimonies of his life. It was special to feel God's presence in the almost 2,000 that were in attendance that day. Dr. F. Bailey Stone, Travis' former pastor, gave a stirring message on the life of Mr. Bryan. It was really special knowing Travis B. Bryan, Jr. was at home with the King of Kings and Lord of Lords, always a WINNER forever.

I don't recall seeing any seagulls flying around the skies of Bryan, Texas, that September day. But, seagulls have been flapping their wings and screeching that call of theirs all these years, as I remember the man who showed me what it was like to walk with Jesus. And to see his life epitomize the "never give up" strength of the Lord indwelling him.

"Lord Jesus, thank You for bringing Travis B. Bryan, Jr. into my life. His impact and influence has lasted 50+ years. He was a mentor You gave me. He was that picture of a man of God who could compete and be compassionate at the same time. He is a reminder of You, Lord Jesus, Who are a friend for Life. Mr. Bryan is a model of one to follow as fighting a good fight, finishing our course, and keeping the faith."

Oh, yes...I hope and pray God sends a Travis B. Bryan, Jr. into your life at just the right moment! And remember this...Truth will always find a way!

Chapter Fifteen

Others - "Those things..."

"Those things, which ye have both learned, and received, and heard,
and seen in me, do: and the God of peace shall be with you."
Philippians 4:9

There are many *others* of whom I have been blessed to have access to their wisdom, and some, their personal mentorship. But from all, they have had a direct impact in my life which has also trickled down to my family and to those I have had the privilege to share the wonderful Life Truths these folks gave to me. I could not finish this beautiful trip back in time without including them, and *those things,* in my recognition of their contribution.

My only concern is that after my manuscript is completed (or, so I will think), I will remember some more that I will regret I didn't think of beforehand. God knows who they are and hopefully will reward them accordingly (and why I didn't think of them before printing this book).

I have decided to put this group in alphabetical order (by their first name or title), so as to not seemingly place an emphasis or importance on one above the other. In whatever way I recall their Truth(s)...*those things*...they shared with me, I am including them because of the impact they and their Truth(s) have made on my life. Thank You, Lord, for these *others.*

Adrian Rogers – (1931 - 2005) the man many said *sounded like God* when he spoke, especially when preaching. A pastor's pastor. Barbara and I started attending Church Training right after we were Born Again at Sagemont Church (Houston, Texas) in May, 1980. The very first Sunday evening we went was the start of the presentation of Adrian Rogers' "What Every Christian Should Know" video series. My goodness, what great Truths we learned from that study. One in particular is what Dr. Rogers pointed out from Genesis that "only Adam and Eve were created, and created in the image of God. Every man and woman after them were begat in the image of Adam." Wow! That changes the discussion. And in

30+ years since, I have rarely heard anyone else EVER say that, since that evening on June 1, 1980. It is incredible the difference between "created" and "begat." ONLY Adam and Eve are the only humans who were ever "created." BUT now, listen! Every Born Again person is "created." Scripture clearly speaks of Believers being a "new creation." THAT is totally different from being "begat."

I have two or three bibles that are chock full of notations where I heard Adrian preach on noted verses, some complete with an outline or notes on what he preached. Another great truth from Adrian I remember first hearing came on August 9, 1983, at the Bring Them In Bus Workers Conference at Broadway Baptist Church, Memphis, Tennessee (my great friend Larry Hipps' ministry…see Larry mentioned later in this chapter): "God does not judge by sin which has been committed (man is born with this), but by the light that has been rejected!" Whew! Want his outline from that sermon? "Romans 1:16-2:12. 1. All men have some light (1:18-20). 2. Light refused increases darkness (v.21). 3. Light obeyed increases light (vs.16-17). 4. Men are going to be judged according to how much light they've received (2: 11-12)." Bonus: "1:20, you can't have a creation without a Creator!" How much light have you received? Tried to obtain? Rejected?

One statement of Dr. Rogers' I remember, and have quoted over and over, is this: "Anything I can talk you into, someone else can talk you out of. But whatever the Holy Spirit convicts you of – is yours forever."

Andrew Murray – (1828 - 1917) the man who was such a prolific writer with a bent toward one idea: edifying believers. Andrew Murray showed me many Truths about the "Love of God." I believe he thought it the most powerful part of God. And when I read his thoughts: "Never can I learn to love until the Spirit of God fills my heart with God's love," I began a search for this filling!

The "points" that impacted my life from Andrew Murray's teachings are far too numerous to write down. I can really only encourage you to grab his books that I list (and his others if you can find them!) and read/re-read/make notes/mark in the margins for easy finding later on/and meditate on the volumes of Truth that God will open to your Soul (the one God gave you at your New Birth). Check out my writings on the Christian's 2nd Soul in my book, *all i want is Jesus! - Vol.1*.

Each of Murray's books will have something especially for you!
Humility
Absolute Surrender

The Power of the Blood of Jesus
Daily Experience With God
Experiencing the Holy Spirit
With Christ In the School of Prayer
Abide In Christ
Like Christ
The Prayer Life
Waiting on God
The Two Covenants

Dave Ramsey – the man thousands have grown to love and enjoy for his unique way of presenting God's financial Truths for a needy, hurting Christian home. Dave is not the first to present some of his ideas (remember, Barbara and I had been living DEBT FREE since 1981, and I was teaching John Morgan's *Financial Freedom Seminar* for years before we ever heard of Dave Ramsey. And many others had learned from Ron Blue, Crown Ministries, Larry Burkett, Suze Orman, to name a few), but he has a style, experience, and some very catchy phrases that drive home the points that are easy to remember and are desirous of following. Dave has one of those grins that just captures his listeners. His *Financial Peace University* has helped thousands of families over the years to get out of the burden and bondage of debt, begin to understand how to take control of their money instead of letting money control them, and work toward LIVING like no one else at a later date by living like no one else in the present…which leads me to share some of my favorite Dave Ramsey quotes:

> "If you will live like no one else; later you can LIVE like no one else."
> "EVERY DOLLAR NEEDS TO HAVE A NAME ON IT!"
> "It's called Plastic Surgery!" (as Dave snaps his huge, oversized scissors on stage…)
> "Turn those fat and flabby expenses into a well-toned budget." "The debt snowball"…a simple plan to get rid of debt that anyone can do.
> "Dumb math and stupid tax"…his designation how most are fooled and misled with typical, worldly money management ideas.
> "Your money needs to work for you, not lie around."
> "We often say that we give the same financial advice your grandmother would, only we keep our teeth in."
> "I am positive that personal finance is 80 percent behavior and only 20 percent head knowledge."

"Live on a budget. Don't spend more than you make. Start an emergency fund. Get out of debt and stay out of debt."

His practical advice is outstanding. Let me illustrate: everyone teaches that individual/families ought to have a budget or spending plan. But Dave came up with this phrase…"every dollar needs to have a name on it." And Dave taught this is to be done BEFORE each month begins! He has taught us a dynamic principle of money management: most people have a good idea of how much money they will have as income for a month, before the month is there. Dave says, "Decide your budget, then NAME every dollar you expect to get during the month, and spend each dollar ONLY as its NAME tells you." This is a simple, practical, uncomplicated method of getting control of your income/outgo. Most people have NO IDEA where their money goes each month. No spending plan, no keeping track of how much they spend and what they spend it on, and they have no idea how they will end the month financially. Dave's "name game" will stop careless, useless, and foolish spending. So, what do Barbara and I do? We don't spend any money that does not have a NAME on it before the month begins!

Thank you, Dave Ramsey, for giving the Christian community (and anyone for that matter!) some fun, basic tools for trusting God for His supply, and living on it. In addition to *Financial Peace University*, let me recommend these two books that I have found helpful (for me and the ones I Coach): *Total Money Makeover,* and *Financial Peace*.

Dr. Hal Boone – (1923 – 2004) Dr. Hal was the Minister of Missions at Sagemont Church in Houston, Texas, when we were Born Again. Later, when I became the Bus & Children's Church Minister/Minister of Evangelism (1983), he and I talked quite a bit about issues people were having, including "doubting their salvation." It was during one of those talks that he gave me a great Truth that I have used many, many times. "Lee," Dr. Hal said, "I believe that it is impossible for a Lost man to 'doubt' his salvation. Only a Saved man/Born Again man will ever doubt his salvation. It is impossible to doubt something that you really don't know the Truth of, or it has never really entered your mind. It is not an option for a lost soul. They simply don't know anything of this."

Actually, Dr. Hal pointed out to me the scripture that best describes how/when a Believer may "doubt" their salvation: 2 Peter 1:5-9. Verse 9 is the focal point of one who "doubts" ("he that lacketh these things is blind, and cannot see afar off, and hath *forgotten* that he was purged from his old sins"). Now, listen, "seeing" our desperate need for forgiveness of sin, Christ's death on His cross as the real and only propitiation for our sin, and the absolute reality that God's salvation is available only through a new birth: these have come only through revelation (God revealing these to us). Another great truth Dr. Hal passed on to me was how unspectacular sincere communication with God should be. I would catch myself raising my head as he prayed, and peeking to see just where God was in the room! Dr. Hal had been a medical doctor in Pasadena (TX) near Sagemont Church, when God called him to be a missionary. He was serving the Lord in Africa when on one trip into the bush he was injured in an automobile accident. It left him paralyzed from the waist down. He lived the rest of his life in a wheelchair, and his wife, Pat, got him around and to & fro for years. It was a privilege to know and spend some great moments with Dr. Hal Boone.

Dr. Robert Lehmann – a renowned eye doctor in Nacogdoches, TX. (Lehmann Eye Center, 5300 North Street, Nacogdoches, TX 75965, 936-569-8278, www.lehmanneyecenter.com). People from all over the world come to see Dr. Lehmann.

Back in August of 2012 he gave me a whole new perspective on the truthful meaning of "seeing." It is like what the man born blind said in John 9:25, "…one thing I know, that, whereas I was blind, now I see." After surgery for cataracts and astigmatism in both eyes, NOW I SEE! I was at the point where I was having difficulty reading with my glasses! Well, Dr. Lehmann said to me, "Lee, when you get tired of coming to me and getting a new prescription for new glasses, let me know. I can put some lenses into your eyes where you will not need any new glasses ever again." I was startled. New eyes? Well, long story short, he operated and put intraocular lens implants into my eyes. "See"???

I laughingly tell everyone I can now "see" the hairs inside a rabbit's nose @ 100 yards! And everything is brighter! The first time I walked into Wal-Mart after the surgery the brightness of their lights frightened me! Wow! "Once I was blind, now I can see!" Now, listen, that's what it is like when God opens our eyes and lets us "see" the Truth of His Word! Dr. Lehmann not only gave me incredible physical eyesight for everyday life (and nighttime too!), but led me to deeper insights into scriptures like Proverbs 20:12, "The hearing ear, and the seeing eye, the LORD hath made even both of them." and Matthew 13:10-17:

> And the disciples came, and said unto Him, Why
> speakest thou unto them in parables? He answered
> and said unto them, Because it is given unto you to

know the mysteries of the kingdom of heaven, but unto them it is not given. For whosoever hath, to him shall be given, and he shall have more abundance: but whosoever hath not, from him shall be taken away even that he hath. Therefore I speak to them in parables: because they seeing see not; and hearing they hear not; neither do they understand. And in them is fulfilled the prophecy of Isaiah, which saith, By hearing ye shall hear, and shall not understand; and seeing ye shall see, and shall not perceive: for this people's heart is waxed gross, and their ears are dull of hearing, and their eyes they have closed; lest at any time they should see with their eyes, and hear with their ears, and should understand with their heart, and should be converted, and I should heal them. But blessed are your eyes, for they shall see: and your ears, for they hear. For verily I say unto you, That many prophets and righteous men have desired to see those things which ye see, and have not seen them; and to hear those things which ye hear, and have not heard them."

Do you "see" what God is giving us in these great verses??? Beautiful!

As of this writing, 6 years later, my "seeing" is still spectacular in the physical, and my "seeing" in the spiritual is increasing. Thank you, Dr. Lehmann! Thank You, God!

Frank Whitaker – a pastor friend since 1982, my second semester in seminary. My family (Barbara, and our two daughters, Kelly and Jennifer) had moved from Houston to Ft. Worth in December, 1981, for me to further my education and training for ministry. (Southwestern had a Houston extension on the campus of Houston Baptist University where I had taken two evangelism classes in the Fall of 1981 with Dr. Roy Fish as my professor. I knew though that I had to go to Ft. Worth to really get into this move to the life of a minister). God gave us a small house close by the seminary to live in.

The same day we were moving in, another family was moving in to a house just down the street. The Garrisons were from Alabama. John & Amelia and their kids had come for John to go to seminary also. Not long after school started for the Spring semester, John and I were in the library between classes one day. A friend of John's from Alabama came and sat down. John introduced me to Frank Whitaker. Frank and I had some similar life experiences in the business world before God called both of us into a life of ministry. I got up from the table and headed out the door to go to the next class. Frank followed me out into the hallway. He said he had heard me say to John that I was looking for a place to do some ministry. Frank told me he lived in Mineral Wells with his family (wife, Carol, and two daughters, Carla and Mona). He was pastoring a small church on the edge of Mineral Wells and going to school. He drove in the 50 miles with a couple of other guys preaching in small churches in that area. He told me, "Lee, if you want to minister, I can give you the opportunity to do all you want to do." He went on to explain he was pastoring a small church where I could teach a young adult SS class that was needed, do some preaching, and lead out in outreach and evangelism. Wow! Sounded great to me. I went home and told Barbara and the girls, and they looked at me like a new-born calf looks at a barbed-wire fence for the first time. But, they were willing to follow me wherever. And for the next 15 months or so, we drove out on Sunday mornings EARLY, then back to Ft. Worth on Sunday nights LATE. But what a great time we had with the Whitakers, the people of Lawn Terrace Baptist Church, and some of the greatest Christians I have known. We led the local association in baptisms for the year! I have recorded in one of my old bibles the names of 3 youth that I baptized. The first baptisms I ever did. I recall doing my first funeral there. I recall our youngest daughter, Jennifer, coming down the aisle one Sunday night at Lawn Terrace after Frank preached, and I was standing there to greet someone coming for prayer or a decision. She wanted to get saved!

The list of biblical Truths Frank taught me, along with the pastoral "truths," have been a huge part of my life for the last 30+ years.

There certainly weren't any actual seagulls flying around the skies in Mineral Wells those days, except for the invisible ones encircling all the Truths of scripture and the truths of ministry that God gave me through my long-time, great friend Frank Whitaker. The memories would encompass a large volume if Frank and I, and our wives (and the girls!) were to sit down and capitulate all that we saw, heard, did, and saw done while at Mineral Wells. Oh, well, I do have to tell you about the front living room floor in the parsonage across the street from the church. It was so "pliable" that only one person could walk across the room at one time, like one of those floating wooden bridges. Well, amen.

Hannah Whitall Smith – (1832 - 1911) the grand lady of Divine inspirations back in the 19th century who shared with all of us the revelations God gave her of the magnitude of Almighty God working in the lives of Christians. Anyone who reads her writings will be blessed beyond measure. Smith's *The Christian's Secret of a Happy Life* was 1st published in 1870. Think about it. It was over 150 years ago that Hannah Whitall Smith was sharing these profound Truths about the grace of God at work in the life of a Christian.

Here are just a few of the wonderful truths I gleaned from Ms. Smith: "Your salvation comes not because your faith saves you, but because it links you to the Savior Who saves." (Ephesians 2:8 makes certain it is the grace of God, what He does, that "saves" us. John 1:12 tells us when we receive, trust in, Christ, God gives us the power to be Born Again.)

"In order to grow in grace, we must first be planted in grace's fruitful soil, tended by a Divine Husbandman, and warmed by the Son of Righteousness, to bring forth much fruit. Grace is the unhindered, wondrous, boundless love of God, poured out upon us in an infinite variety of ways by His measureless heart of love. To grow in grace means being planted in the very heart of this Divine love, to put ourselves in His hands and leave it with Him."

"Man's part is to trust. God's part is to work." (bold, my emphasis)

"Doubting God is sin. It is blasphemy."

"It is never a sign of Divine leading when the Christian insists on battering down doors the Lord has not opened."

"God's promise is that He will take possession of our will and work in us to do His will."

all from: *The Christian's Secret of a Happy Life* & *The God of All Comfort*

Ian Thomas – (1914 - 2007) getting to meet Ian Thomas was a huge thrill. I had read some of his books and took one to get him to autograph! It was at a church in College Station, Texas, where I had gone to college almost 25 years before. Ian Thomas has written some of the most profound words that Christians have ever read. His books are chock full of the incredible Truths emanating from great Life Verses. Thomas was a master of declaring the Life of Christ of Colossians 1:27: "To whom God would make known what is the riches of the glory of this mystery among the Gentiles; which is Christ in you, the hope of glory."

Our Life, Thomas would often declare, is not a Life of inactivity but of Christ-activity. It is not what you can do for God, but what He can do through you. "It is all in Christ, you see; and all of Christ is yours! Would you be willing to surrender everything and pray, 'I do not want any other program, any other kind of life, but the one that You Yourself are prepared to live in and through me'?"

His three books: *The Saving Life of Christ, The Mystery of Godliness*, and *The Indwelling Life of Christ* have all made a great impact on my life, and those I minister to. Here are a few of the major helps Thomas gave to me:

- We are reconciled to God by Christ's death. We are saved by Christ's Life.
- It is only the Life of the Lord Jesus – His activity, clothed with you and displayed through you - that ultimately will find the approval of God.
- Sometimes the severest penalty that God can inflict upon His people who reject what they need is to give them what they want. In defiance of God's Word, God's mind, God's will, and God's judgment, they tried to discern between good and bad in what God had totally rejected.
- Do not be dull in spiritual hearing, sluggish & slothful in achieving spiritual insights, inexperienced & unskilled in the doctrine of righteousness.
  (on pgs 121-122, The Saving Life of Christ) the WHAT, the WHY, the HOW of ALL spiritual activity.

Jack Taylor – I had one of those "iconic" moments in Jack Taylor's presence just 4 months after being Born Again. Jack Taylor was a renowned pastor and biblical teacher who was at a bible conference at a church in League City, Texas, where an old high-school friend, Everett Nix, was pastor, with whom I had just reconnected 15 years after graduation. He was the pastor; I was a new Believer. He invited me to come to a pastor's meeting and luncheon where Jack was going to be speaking to some pastors. I was the only non-pastor present. In a 25-30 minute ministry to 13-15 pastors I remember one thing in particular Jack Taylor told these men, "Guys, preach the Word of God, and don't worry about the consequences. If the people of your church do not want to hear God, let them run you off or whatever. Just remember this: you are God's man, and He will have another place for you." As I walked out of that meeting, for the life of me (no pun intended. God was speaking to His

Life in me!), I had no idea why I thought these thoughts that ran through my mind: "Wow! That is a good word to these men. I bet that is so encouraging."

Little did I know at that moment Jack Taylor's words were as much for me as the other men in the room. That day I had NO IDEA God would be calling me to be a pastor within the next year. At that moment, I had NO IDEA of the challenges I would face in EVERY church I pastored, or served as an interim or part-time pastor. (My pastor, John Morgan, told me when we were discussing my call to ministry: "Lee, make sure it is God calling you. You will face times when IF God has not called you, you will pack up and leave.")

Thank you, Jack Taylor, for the words years before that have served as a reminder, an encouragement, an emboldenment, and a comfort when a trial of rebellious members came calling. Over and over I had peace from God that I know was a remembrance of His words spoken through Jack Taylor back in 1980. A big "thank you" to Bro. John and Bro. Jack: God has not let me leave.

Two of Jack Taylor's books: *The Key To Triumphant Living*, & *The Hallelujah Factor* have given me many great helps to enjoying Christ, and here are a couple of the major ones:

- God spoke to me, "It's Jesus, only, that you need to Live the Life I require and you desire."
- While Christ's death for us secures our relationship, our death with Him procures our fellowship.
- God has an affinity for praise. He is at home in praise.
- The absence of praise simply means that someone has an inadequate view of God. To know Him is to praise Him.
- Knowing that the Holy Spirit is resident in your life, ask Him to be the reigning Lord of your life.
- To be "filled with the Spirit" means that we are to be controlled, guided, and motivated by the same Holy Spirit.

Jack Taylor makes several monumental statements about "praise" in his 1974 book, *The Hallelujah Factor*, regarding what is a "sound mind" and an "insane mind":

- "Problems that had haunted me were solved in Christ: depression and discouragement, removed by the therapy of thanksgiving…distress, also removed by the therapy of thanksgiving… deficiency and defeat, by the therapy of praise."
- "The seeds of insanity are in sin. Insanity proliferates in a praiseless atmosphere."

- "The process from sanity to insanity occurs when one turns from praising God to praising self."
- "It is time that in an age of increasing pressures and multiplications of threats to life on earth, we adopt praise as life-style for the preservation of mental balance."
- "Eternity alone will reveal how many people populate the (mental) institutions of our land and world who are there because of the absence of praise – and who stay there because praise is not introduced." (YES, this was in 1974!)

How wonderful it is these days to be sitting by the dock of the bay, or wading in the calm surf on the Gulf Coast, watching the sun rise and the birds starting to fly around, seagulls included! All the while enjoying Christ's Sound Mind of peaceful and fruitful thoughts filled with praise of God, instead of sitting slumped down in a chair somewhere in an institution due to having lived with praise of self, discouragement, depression, and despair.

Thank God, for those divine appointments with John and Jack way back when…

Larry Hipps – Larry Hipps has been a great co-servant in ministry (in one capacity or another) for almost 40 years! I was at Southwestern Seminary in Ft. Worth, TX, when Sagemont Church called me to be their Bus & Children's Church Minister and Minister of Evangelism (Aug., 1983). Before I ever set foot in the bus ministry office at Sagemont, Bro. Bill Moore, Assoc. Pastor (who had started the bus ministry at Sagemont), sent me to Memphis, Tennessee (to Broadway Baptist Church), to a Bring Them In Conference (Larry's ministry) to see first-hand what the bus ministry and children's church was all about.
What a monumental few days!

Not only did I get to meet Larry, his wife, Cathy, see how they did children's church, bus ministry, and other children's ministry, and gather some practical & extremely helpful materials, but I met and heard three men who gave me some tremendous Truths to carry with me for the rest of my ministry and life: (1) Adrian Rogers, "The Righteousness of God" (Romans 1:16-21) (2) Jerry Falwell, "Seek Ye First" (Matthew 6:33), and (3) Jimmy Ervin, "Child Conversion" (Matthew 18:1-6, 10-14). I learned the bus ministry and children's church ministry from Larry Hipps and Bring Them In (BTI). Larry Hipps has helped more churches (and those who work with children in all areas of ministry) around the world than most would ever dream of doing.

One comment I love to make about Larry is this: "Larry Hipps has forgotten more than most children's ministry workers will ever know!" Over the years I have had Larry come to the churches I was pastoring and do a BTI conference or workshop. He has brought folks who also do children's ministry. But, Bro. Larry has always given my workers (and any from other churches who were attending) some of the most powerful ideas and tools for sharing the Gospel. One of the best of his great materials is his 2-year study of bible characters and stories. 104 Sundays of the most detailed, outlined, inclusive facts, figures, crafts, and interactive games that any teacher/preacher could want. I used those two books for my Sunday morning messages to two different groups in Children's Church while the Bus Minister at Sagemont. The kids loved every one!

I do have a bone to pick with Larry. Because of a little challenge the Children's Church of Sagemont had with the Children's Church of Broadway, in order to encourage our kids to bring more visitors and set an all-time attendance record, we had a "Make Bro. Lee Kiss The Pig Day." Two of the most precious saints I have ever known are Fred and Karen Saltsman. They were the organizers and leaders of Sagemont's Childrens Church ministry. I am not sure to this day just how involved they were in this "small matter." Well, this "small matter" was this: we had over 1,000 ride the buses to Sagemont that day. And the little piglet the bus and childrens church workers had shown me when we started promoting the Day, well, it turned into a 250lb monster pig (stank to High Heaven, no pun intended!) that I ended up kissing in front of the whole church on the gym stage after the morning service that day, getting close to its snout at the cage's side! Kiss the PIG! Larry, I never used that idea again!

Oh, how I wish I had known of the seagulls during that time. I bet there are some phenomenal Seagull Promotional Sundays a church near the coast could come up with!

Manley Beasley – (1932 - 1990) the man who could look "through you" while looking straight at you, and his smile warmed your heart. What a joy to have met and to have been around Bro. Manley a few times. He had a special gift of giving someone a certain "importance," even though he wasn't a great friend, didn't spend much time with you, perhaps really didn't know your name. His walk with God was different from most Christians. It always seemed he was more intimate with God than most.

I don't recall how many times I heard him speak, how many of his books and materials I read or still possess, but each moment in fellowship with him personally seems like it was a moment of God giving me some new revelation or confirmation. His piercing, attentive look was really meaningful. I love his friend Ron Owen's statement about Manley: "the fragrance of the Life of Christ pressed through his humanity."
Whew!

His message over and over was really: "Believe God." And that when we REALLY do BELIEVE God, we will see His Faith become the link between us and God. Manley Beasley was God's gift to many pastors who needed the encouragement and solid guidance to a more personal fellowship with God. God's Faith was his mantra. What it is, how we got it, what it would do for us.

Some quotes about "faith" from Bro. Manley that have been helpful to me:

- "Faith is acting as if it is so when it is not so in order for it to become so because God says it is so."
  I can't tell you how many people I have heard "quote" Bro. Manley's statement, BUT, most do not mention the last 6 words, which are the crux of his statement! When God has said it is so, and we believe God, then His Faith enables us to "act" the rest of what Manley has stated!
- "True faith bids eternal Truth to become present reality."
- "Faith does not always take you out of the storm but it will calm you in the storm."
- "God showed me there are three elements to Bible faith: intellectual, emotional, and volitional."
  (in a crucial moment in Manley's life) "I came to the conclusion I had rather fail, trusting Jesus, than to sit there and doubt. I said sink or swim, live or die, I'm going to trust God."
- "A man must believe before he can receive."

Perhaps the most sought after work of Manley Beasley is his *Faith Is* Workbook. It is a lengthy, uncomplicated, practical, and powerful look at what God showed Bro. Manley through his studies, his life's experiences, and his experiencing God. I believe EVERY Christian should own this book, and OWN the Truths within it.

Barbara and I had the privilege and pleasure of spending a few moments with Bro. Manley in his office in North Texas. I was a student at Southwestern Seminary in Ft. Worth, and we drove to his office to get some materials. Bro. Manley was in the office that day. While we were there, he came out and talked with us briefly. I don't know of words that adequately tell of the power of God engulfing us during that visit.

We also remember the last time we saw him. It was in New Orleans, June, 1990, at the Super Dome, where the Southern Baptist Convention was being held. That, too, is a special memory. He went home with the Lord the next month.

Oswald Chambers (1874 – 1917) the man who has been a great friend of preachers and teachers from a little over 100 years ago. His devotional, *My Utmost for His Highest*, is a classic. One thing interesting about Chambers, he spoke more about "abiding" and "grace" than most, yet many of his readers who love and recommend his book to others, do not observe the "abiding" or "grace" teaching. Why is that? Why is it that so many Christians read, go to conferences, attend bible studies, and then keep on "working" instead of "abiding" and living in "God's grace"? I have a simple answer: faulty definitions. That's right, when someone reads the practical, uncomplicated teachings of Oswald Chambers through the lens of faulty definitions then they see a message that is not what Oswald has given. "Abiding" and "grace" in most Christians' minds are nebulous thoughts wrapped up in some mystical idea of whom their God is. It is like "saved" and "born again." One tends to "begat" a whole host of weak Believers, while the other "creates" Rock-solid Believers. The former is because of man's ideas, and the latter is from the heart of God. Friend, you may not be sure whether you have been "saved," or not, BUT you KNOW if you have been "Born Again," or not! And Oswald Chambers' teachings on "abiding" and "grace" are clear, precise, and understandable to the Spiritual mind. Oh, wait a minute, that unravels a whole new box of misunderstandings.

Someone gave Barbara and me our first copy of *My Utmost for His Highest* way back in the early 1980's, shortly after we were Born Again. We currently have about 4 or 5 copies in our possession, all marked, underlined, highlighted, with notes in any margin available. We have given away several copies. He was an "almost" choice to be an addition to one of the first 14 chapters of this book. Over the years, WE HAVE SPENT SEVERAL HOURS READING THROUGH THIS BOOK. Over and over Oswald Chambers has given us so much insight into the Truths of the Holy Scriptures.

I even found a copy of *Oswald Chambers: Abandoned to God* (The Life Story of Oswald Chambers) by David McCasland. I highly recommend this book to anyone who has any desire to KNOW the man behind *My Utmost for His Highest*.

For the Christian wanting to delve into the depths of spiritual Truths, spend time in the Index in the last pages of MUfHH. There you will find words that grab your heart, and a list of page numbers where you can quickly go to Oswald Chambers' own revelations from God about the topic. See if God quickens your Spirit just as He did Mr. Chambers'.

Some of the words (phrases) of which Chambers gave much meaning to me were:

abandonment - abiding - atonement - belief - born again - Christ in me - concentration on God - crisis - Cross of Christ - dependence on God - devotion to Jesus - discipleship - discipline - depression - experience - faith - friendship with God - grace of God - hearing God - holiness - Holy Spirit - humility - identification - intimacy with Jesus - joy - looking to God - love - natural (man) - obedience - obstinacy - patience - poverty of spirit - prayer - purpose of God - redemption - redemptive reality - regeneration - right relationship - Rivers of Living Water - sacrifice - sanctification – self - simplicity of relationship - sinner made saint - suffering - unbelief - vision - wait on God - walk in the Light - will of God - wisdom of God - worry

Words have meaning. Correct definitions are the critical first step in using words to convey what we intend to convey.

For the Christians wanting the most of Oswald Chambers, check out these other writings of his that are very powerful:

Approved Unto God
Conformed to His Image
God's Workmanship
The Love of God
Not Knowing Where
The Philosophy of Sin

Spiros Zodhiates (1922 – 2009) the man thousands and thousands of preachers and bible teachers depend upon for a more accurate and complete understanding of the Greek and Hebrew languages and the words behind the English translation of the New and Old Testaments. Knowing the exact original language word translated into the English is crucial.

As I have mentioned, I am one who believes so strongly that we rise or fall depending on the definitions we possess and use of any and every word we read, hear, or write. Words have meanings, and it is impossible to accurately convey what you intended to say if you don't use the correct word, AND if your hearers or readers don't know and understand the words you use. Being introduced to Spiros Zodhiates took my studies two steps deeper: (1) the Hebrew and Greek words translated into our English language are of crucial importance to know. Translations from ANY text of a foreign language MUST be accurate to the original language. But, (2) the grammar of every language is also crucial to know. Zodhiates is one of the FEW linguists who provides bible students with not only the crucial accurate translations, but including the grammar of the words being translated with all the nuances that are just as crucial. Without such help I am not sure that any English reader can fully and accurately know what they are thinking IS the "Word" of God.

I have three of Zodhiates' books that help me in every endeavor to know, use, and convey what GOD has said in His Word. His *Hebrew-Greek Key Word Study Bible* in the King James Version is the bedrock of bible reading and study for me. But, Zodhiates compiled two companion grammar books that expand the understanding of the New Testament: *The Complete Word Study New Testament* has all the words in the text numerically coded to Strong's Greek Concordance, along with numerous personal notes and grammatical codes on the text, Lexical aides, and Strong's Greek dictionary. *The Complete Word Study Dictionary New Testament* is a complete dictionary of every Greek New Testament word. The depth of Spiros Zodhiates' knowledge and understanding of the Greek language put forth in this book is an incredible assistance to an understanding and use of the text of the New Testament for preachers, teachers, and all bible students. All three of these are available from AMG Publishers, Chattanooga, TN.

My pastor, John Morgan, Sagemont Church, Houston, Texas, told me in 1981 that I should get all I could from Spiros Zodhiates. Knowing the original languages behind the English is vitally important for any accuracy of knowing the Word of God. I thank God for John Morgan's instructions about Spiros Zodhiates.

Barbara and I had the privilege of meeting Spiros Zodhiates a little over 15 years ago at a church in north Houston. Among the numerous grand statements he made in that day or two of speaking, I guess the most startling statement was this: "I have been using and studying the Greek language for over 80 years…and I am still learning something new all the time." Spiros Zodhiates was born to Greek parents on the island of Cyprus in 1922.

I would guess that I have spent hundreds of hours under the "tutelage" of Spiros Zodhiates, and I am grateful to God for every minute. I could not encourage you enough to contact AMG Publishers and get any and all of Zodhiates' books. In addition to the three mentioned, here are a few commentaries that I possess and surely recommend:

The Beatitudes; Faith Love & Hope (study of the Book of James)
1 Corinthians 1, A Richer Life For You In Christ
1 Corinthians 2, A Revolutionary Mystery
1 Corinthians 4, Seeking The Praise Of God
1 Corinthians 9, Victory Through Discipline
1 Corinthians 15, Conquering The Fear of Death

Now listen, Zodhiates is not the ONLY language scholar that I have books from, study, reference, etc. There are many language scholars who add immense helps to gleaning the correct words, correct nuances, correct meanings...but Spiros Zodhiates has been my "bedrock" scholar I turn to. I can't imagine any Bible student, teacher, or preacher who doesn't have and use as many "helps" as are available.

Steve McVey – a man who as a pastor knew something was missing in the connection of his church members and God, and whom God showed that missing link in a marvelous way. I wish I could remember who introduced me to, or how I was made aware of, Steve McVey and his pastoral perspectives on grace. As a pastor, I find his "pastoral" thoughts and explanations with illustrations very helpful to use in communicating the work of Christ in our life.

Like so many Believers, I knew the common definition of grace to be this: "God's unmerited favor." I believed that. But, tell me, WHAT does ANY Christian possess, as a Christian, that isn't "God's unmerited favor"??? I firmly believe that EVERYTHING I have received from God is not because I deserved it in any way, but He has given it to me as a gift, undeserved. However, how does a Christian "grow in grace" as 2 Peter 3:18 says,

"But grow in grace, and in the knowledge of our Lord and Savior Jesus Christ."

The Greek *auxano* (grow) carries with it "to enlarge, to give the increase." How does a Christian DO that if it is "God's unmerited favor"? Or, "be strong in grace" as 2 Timothy 2:1 says,

> "Thou therefore, my son, be strong in the grace that is in Christ Jesus."

The Greek *endunamoo* (to be strong) carries with it "to make strong, vigorous, to be strengthened." How does the Christian DO that if it is "God's unmerited favor"?

So, for many years I wrestled with this until the day I was reading McVey's *Grace Walk*. And God really opened my mind to the fact that grace is "something God does for me." Yes, I knew Colossians 3:3-4, "For ye are dead, and your life is hid with Christ in God. When Christ, who is our life, shall appear, then shall ye also appear with Him in glory."

But, you know how something just sort of grabs you somewhere along life's path, something you have known or been aware of, but you just didn't KNOW it. There was this moment that God said to me, "Lee, what I have been trying to get you to own is that the Life you now have is not your own, it is Christ's, and you are living but it is HIM wanting to Live His Life through you."

The law meant that I had to do something for God. I had lived for many, many years not so much under the bondage of the law regarding salvation, but in order to "be a good Christian" I was still there. All of a sudden I no longer was under that bondage. I no longer HAD to, I GOT to enjoy Christ's Life in and through me as a Christian. And, so Steve, Michael Wells, Watchman Nee, and many others started getting my attention as to how much the scriptures pointed out "what God has done for me," and "what God will do for me." And that God loved me if I never did another thing for Him. I know I had heard these things before, but now I OWNED them!

Let me tell you. You need to get Steve McVey's books:

> *Grace Walk*
> *Grace Land*
> *Grace Rules*
> *A Divine Invitation*
> *and The Godward Gaze*

Not many folks can convey the truths of God's work IN and THROUGH the Christian like Steve McVey.

Watchman Nee – (1903-1972) a man God penned many books through. Each one has been a big seller and major influence in the lives of millions of Christians. I appreciate getting to know some of his best words to Believers.

Watchman Nee gave me many outstanding insights and definitions of key spiritual words. I love definitions, accurate Truthful definitions. As Michael Wells used to always say, "We rise and fall on our definitions." And Gary Ezzo always said, "Say what you mean, and mean what you say." Here are a couple of my most favorite definitions from Nee:

- revelation – "What constitutes a revelation by the Holy Spirit? Revelation enables us to see what God sees. All things are naked and laid bare before Him. Any covering is upon our eyes, not God's. When God opens our eyes that we may know the intent of our heart and the deepest thought within us in the measure that He Himself knows us – this is revelation. As we are naked and laid bare before Him, so are we before ourselves as we receive revelation. This is revelation: for us to be allowed to see what our Lord sees. Whenever you are enabled to discern the thoughts and intents of your heart, you can be sure your soul and spirit are being divided." (*The Release of the Spirit*, pgs.72-73).

- brokenness – "We should ask ourselves, what impression do I give to others? How often we have emphasized the need for our outward man to be broken. If this brokenness is not accomplished, others meet the impact of our outward man. Whenever we are in their presence they are made uncomfortable by our self-love, or pride, or obstinacy, or cleverness, or eloquence. But is God being satisfied? If God is not satisfied, and the church is not helped, any impression we leave is for naught. Beloved, God's full intention requires that our spirit be released." (Nee makes certain throughout his book to identify this "outward" part of Born Again man as the Natural Soul the Christian was born with as a Lost Sinner, but retains after the New Birth) (*The Release of the Spirit*, pg.76).

One thing that is really impressive about Watchman Nee's teaching is his constant reference to and demand to see the difference between man's soul and spirit; however, I wish he had distinguished between Lost Man and Born Again Man (there is no "man" since the Fall and Redemption of Adam and Eve) AND that Born Again Man has 2 souls (The natural soul from his physical birth and Christ's Soul given to him at his Spiritual Birth/New Birth/Born Again).

Nee's teaching of "The Blood of Christ" in the 1st chapter of his book, *The Normal Christian Life*, along with the 2nd chapter, "The Cross of Christ," opened the door for me to see so much of what these two offered and gave to me, plus seeing the different value of each to me. Here are my notes from an open space between the two chapters of the paperback I have devoured over and over:

- the Blood deals with what we have done. the Cross deals with what we are.
- we need the Blood for forgiveness. we need the Cross for deliverance.
- the Blood deals with sins. the Cross deals with sinners.

And these are two magnificent testimonies:

- the Cross...death...I in Christ
- the Resurrection...Life...Christ in me

Not all will agree with everything Watchman Nee writes, including myself, but he constantly dealt with the "deeper, spiritual" things of Christianity and not with the flesh and surface issues (which the Church seems to be constantly preoccupied with).

Here are some of Nee's books that I have and enjoy:

The Normal Christian Life
The Release of the Spirit
Spiritual Authority
The Spiritual Man
Not I But Christ
Full of Grace and Truth
Spirit of Wisdom and Revelation

I thank God for these Saints in Chapter 15 who have given me many more of "those things" that have enabled me to receive His Life as My Life and enjoy His peace! The many Truths gleaned through these Saints, may they be as meaningful to you.

Lord Jesus, thank You for ALL the "Others" You have given to me revealing Your Truth and Your ways. Thank You for always bringing to light You and Your Truth. May You bring many "Others" to show Yourself plain and clear, precise and complete, each and every time I need Truth.

Oh yes...I hope and pray God sends multiple "Others" into your life at just the right moment! Truth will always find a way!

Chapter Sixteen

Truth Creates Faithfulness – "Commit thou to faithful men"

"And the things that thou hast heard of me among many
witnesses, the same commit thou to faithful men, who shall be
able to teach others also."
2 Timothy 2:2

I love this verse. I remember its impact while in my first semester of
seminary in a class ("Personal Evangelism") of Professor Dr. Roy Fish.
Dr. Fish pointed out the "4 generations" of "faithful" Christians who are
part of passing along God's Word from "faith to faith." It speaks plainly
of the Apostle Paul telling young Timothy to go forward in ministry and
find those whom God will give him that will be "faithful" learners and
sharers of the Truths Timothy has heard, received, learned, and lived
from the apostle himself. Immediately, we see that Paul considered
Timothy one of those he calls "faithful."

The Greek word translated "faithful" is *pistos*, meaning worthy to be
believed, trustworthy, observant of and steadfast to one's trust/word/ or
promises. This is a profound word. It is vital to know and understand the
implications behind Paul's admonition and instruction to his young
student who is now involved in personal ministry with others. Finding
"faithful" mentees is one of the greatest challenges any pastor, teacher,
or all mentors of any kind will ever fully experience. In almost 40 years
of ministry, I believe I could count only a miniscule number that I
KNOW have proven to be "faithful" in respect to the teaching of 2
Timothy 2:2.

Why is that? God tells us in Mark 4:14-20, as Jesus explained the
Parable of the Sower to His disciples…

> "The sower soweth the word. And these are they by the
> way side, where the word is sown; but when they have
> heard, Satan cometh immediately, and taketh away the
> word that was sown in their hearts. And these are they
> likewise which are sown on stony ground; who, when
> they have heard the word, immediately receive it with

gladness; And have no root in themselves, and so endure but for a time: afterward, when affliction or persecution ariseth for the word's sake, immediately they are offended. And these are they which are sown among thorns; such as hear the word, and the cares of this world, and the deceitfulness of riches, and the lusts of other things entering in, choke the word, and it becometh unfruitful. And these are they which are sown on good ground; such as hear the word, and receive it, and bring forth fruit, some thirtyfold, some sixty, and some a hundred."

It's quite simple, isn't it? The heart (or, soil) of every one dictates the response and fruitfulness in the hearer. It is interesting to say the least that (as grandmas used to say) "the proof is in the pudding."

One thing I vividly remember of those earliest days with John Morgan as our family's pastor at Sagemont Church in Houston, he always was quick and willing to share a great pastor/teacher with the whole church family. That included preachers, teachers, singers, evangelists (all in person at the church), on video cassette (that was the electronic age of that time!), or giving announcement that those would be somewhere in the near vicinity or even at a state conference/revival/etc. That is how I first heard Billy Graham, Bill Gothard, Manley Beasley, Bill Stafford, John McKay, Bailey Smith, Carlos McLeod, Jerry Vines, W. A. Criswell, Adrian Rogers, Charles Stanley, Jimmy Draper, Roy Fish, George Harris, Vance Havner, J. Harold Smith, David Walker, Medford Hudson, Willa Dorsey, and many more that just aren't coming to mind right now. What powerful proclamations of God's Holy Word were given to me because John Morgan was not into building his own kingdom but into building the Kingdom of God. I have always been quick to try and follow the example John Morgan gave to me as a pastor/teacher who had the best interests of his flock at heart.

And so, as I come near the end of this book, I have asked some to share their testimony of faithfulness, their testimony of how God spoke to them a word of Truth many years ago that has impacted their life, their family's life, and even today is impacting some of their grandkids. These testimonies are from some Truth God gave me, or from some of my mentors that I encouraged these folks to seek, listen to, and learn from that ultimately impacted them. What an incredible joy to be coming to this time in my life, all these years later, hearing the stories of those God gave me to disciple who have proven to be one of the "faithful ones."

138

It is my privilege to have been a part of these Saints' lives, to see some of what God has accomplished through their "good ground" hearts and their lives. Listen to them as they tell of the moments they remember God speaking to them. Listen to the moments they remember becoming a *pistis* Christian. Listen to them share the impact of the Word of God in their personal, family, work, or extended life. And listen to them as they speak of how they are experiencing being "worthy to be believed, trustworthy, observant of and steadfast to one's trust/word/ or promises." And listen to them as they share the joy of "teaching others also" who will be found "faithful" in the years to come.

This is a profound chapter in an exposition of how spectacular our great God is, and that Truth creates faithfulness.

Chad & Kelly Graff

Kelly is our oldest daughter. Chad and Kelly met while in college at East Texas Baptist University in Marshall, Texas. She and Chad were married in 1992. They both graduated from ETBU. Kelly teaches at Hallsville High School, Hallsville, Texas. Chad has worked for several years for the State of Texas.

They have two kids: Darby, our oldest granddaughter who turned 24 in August of this year, is the Asst. Volleyball coach at East Texas Baptist University. Darby graduated from Texas A&M University in College Station, TX (my alma mater AND that of my grandfather, O. B. Bradford) and played on the Aggie volleyball team. She also did one year of graduate studies at Arkansas State University in Jonesboro, AR, and played on the Red Wolves volleyball team. Garrett, our third oldest grandchild, who turned 20 in April of this year, is now a junior at East Texas Baptist University in Marshall, TX. He played football, baseball, and was on the track team at Hallsville High School.

Kelly has grown up to be one of the strongest Christian ladies we know. Chad has been the Christian man, husband, and father that we knew God was providing for Kelly. Darby and Garrett are strong Christians who make us most proud and thankful to God.

Their story of Truth that God brought to their lives is great. Truth always finds a way. We could not be more proud of Kelly and Chad & Darby and Garrett! Truth creates faithfulness.

"There is nothing that the nearness of Christ cannot overcome." - Michael Wells

If you are like me, life has had its share of things - some good and some not. Early in my Christian faith, I viewed trials as something I had to overcome and sometimes I felt alone in trying to overcome them.

Later in life, Dad and Mom shared with me (and my young family at the time) the ministry of Michael Wells and ALMI. The concept of abiding really wasn't new because we already knew the scripture in John 15 about the Vine and branches ... but the understanding of true abiding came alive through the lessons heard from Michael.

Real understanding of peace and joy comes from knowing you are not alone in anything you face - triumphs or trials - if your focus is on God and not the situation.

Fast forward to late 2015-2016 when our daughter was battling a health condition that was draining the very life from her even as we tried every possible earthly measure to heal her. There were times when I was focused on the current trial and fear crept in. But God is faithful and He helped me correct my focus. In so many moments, Christ's nearness was palpable as He answered prayers in ways that there was no refuting (by myself or others whom Christ was ministering to in the moment) that He was in control. Peace in the midst of a series of life changing major surgeries was found as I rested in the nearness of Christ. I am thankful to say that I also witnessed the peace that comes from abiding in Christ in my daughter's life (and husband and son) as we walked through this trial together.

It is in abiding in Christ that we are able to make each step forward each day. It is the nearness of Christ which allows us to find peace and joy in life.

Kelly Graff

Braxton & Jennifer Hickman

Jennifer is our youngest daughter. Braxton and Jennifer met while in college at San Jacinto Jr. College in Houston, Texas. Braxton went on to graduate from the University of Texas, while Jennifer graduated from the University of Houston. She and Braxton were married in 1994.

They have two kids: Braden, our oldest grandson who turned 22 in July of this year, is a senior at Colorado State University in Fort Collins, CO. Braden was the starting center on his Seven Lakes High School football team. He will graduate from CSU this December. And Ashleigh, our youngest grandchild, turned 18 in January of this year and recently graduated from Seven Lakes High School in Katy, TX, and started college this Fall at Belmont University in Nashville, TN. Ashleigh played volleyball in high school until a foot injury sent her in a different direction. She joined the newspaper staff at SLHS and became a co-editor-in-chief of the *Torch* school magazine and won several awards as a newspaper journalist.

Jennifer has also grown up to be one of the strongest Christian ladies we know. Braxton has been the Christian man, husband, and father that we knew God was providing for Jennifer. Braden and Ashleigh are strong Christians who make us most proud and thankful to God.

Their story of Truth that God brought to their lives is great. Truth makes us free. We could not be more proud of Jennifer and Braxton & Braden and Ashleigh. Truth creates faithfulness.

My parents attended a couples' conference in Colorado Springs, Colorado, back in 1998 where the speaker, Michael Wells, introduced to them and the participants one of his books. Their being impressed by what they heard and read moved them to share this book with me and my husband.

The most life-changing information that was ever shared with Braxton and me was the teaching of Michael Wells on the Abiding Life. Before that time, I floundered around wondering what God's will for my life was and constantly seeking what would make me believe that I was in His will. No matter what "works" I performed, I was always lacking that inner peace of truly knowing for what God created me.

My introduction to the Abiding Life was through Michael Wells' book Sidetracked in the Wilderness. *I couldn't put it down. There were so many truths packed in each chapter that it was almost overwhelming, but also extremely enlightening and freeing all at the same time! What a blessing!*

First, I learned that God created me and loves me no matter what I do or don't do. For me, that freed up the idea that I had to be doing "works" in order to please God and helped me to understand that "works" are my tribute to God in prayerful thanksgiving for all He has done for me and for loving me unconditionally! As a person, this realization also carries over to help me love others unconditionally…although I am not as consistent as I would like to be. I still have a standard God set as to how to truly love others unconditionally, because they are God's creation just like me.

Second, and probably my favorite insight, I learned that scripture memory is not a thing to be merely recited but should be lived. Knowing God's Word and relying on the Holy Spirit to bring to mind that knowledge when needed is what God intended. Not a recitation without application. Therefore Bible Study becomes a way to know what God has to say on all things. Prayer becomes a tool to help ask God to continue to show us His thoughts in all areas of life through recalling scriptures each day as we live and face any situation. It was revolutionary to my Christian life!

Third, and most importantly, Michael Wells himself says that we should not follow his teaching blindly without question. He taught that our confusion with something that he says helps us to rely on GOD alone in our quest for the truth as

God would apply it to our lives. This helps us to always focus on God and not man. I have applied this to all teachings that I have encountered. They are man's retelling of God's truth for that person. I may or may not be in that place in my life to understand that truth, so it helped me to understand that I must focus on what God has for me in the place that I am at that time in my life. It also helps me to understand why others may not understand a truth I am trying to share...they may not be there yet.

Those are just a few of the truths that I have applied to my life. So many more truths are packed in <u>Sidetracked in the Wilderness</u> as well as all the other books authored by Michael Wells.

Jennifer Hickman

Brian & Jill Davis

I first met Brian and Jill around 25 years ago. We have been close friends for the entire time, enjoying visits in the various states the Davises have lived since leaving Houston. That includes some vacation time hiking Mt. Rainier, seeing the Mt. St. Helens observatory in Washington state, and a trip over to Vancouver and Vancouver Island (Victoria & Butchart Gardens). I have already mentioned how we first met in chapter eight.

With both families having two daughters, our families have been through many similar situations. Interesting that Barbara and I did not know Gary and Anne Marie Ezzo when our kids were the same age as the Davis girls when we went through that *Growing Kids God's Way* study back in the 90's. I would have certainly done a lot of things differently as husband and father than I did in the 70's.

I have always called Brian the "best witness at work" of any Christian I have ever known. I also have always called him "my best friend." It has been a great joy for the past 20+ years to see Brian and Jill Davis be the Christians they give witness to. Listen as they share a couple of things God has shown them. Truth creates faithfulness.

I became a Christian at the age of 14 after a missionary came to our small Church in Maryland and gave his testimony. He began with a simple chalk drawing depicting man's separation from God and how we were "dead" in our sins, lost and without hope. And how, one day, according to Scripture, we would die and spend eternity either in Heaven or Hell. At the age of 14, I knew I didn't want to be cast into any lake on fire! That night, I believed that Jesus is the Son of God and placed my trust in Him.

As the years passed, I was an on again, off again Christian. After a few bad church experiences, questions began to creep in like, am I "good" enough to be a Christian? What's my purpose? Why do I run from the One who saved me? Why does everybody in church seem perfect? After moving to Houston, Texas, in the early 90's my wife, Jill, began looking for a new Church home to attend with our youngest daughters. Our oldest daughter Allison had started the AWANA program at our church in Baltimore, MD, prior to our moving to Houston. Allison loved the program and so did we, so we purposed to find a church in Houston with the program, and that is how God led us to Anchor Baptist Church and the preaching of Pastor Lee McDowell.

Being a good husband, I followed Jill to church. A week later, a knock on the door and there stood Pastor Lee and his wife Barbara. This meant one thing, Jill had filled out the "visitor card!" Now if you are a church hopper like I was, this is a no-no. However, we had a great visit, some laughter and then it was over. Only it wasn't. Next Sunday after the service, Lee invited Jill and me and the girls over for lunch. As I was formulating my excuse, Jill readily said OK! So, that week we drove over to the "Pastor's" home where Lee was grilling some sort of delicious seafood on the grill! We had a nice dinner, good conversation and we left for home and I thought, well that's done. Except it wasn't. Not long after, I was out in the Houston humidity mowing my grass. As I was mowing near the street, a green car with blacked out windows rolls up next to me…and stops. It kind of creeped me out a bit. I shut off the mower, and I could hear the muffled sound of country music playing on the inside of the car. I'm pretty sure it was Reba McIntire. The passenger window rolled down, the music blared out and there with a big Texas smile on his face was Pastor Lee! My first thought was here's a Pastor listening to secular music! I didn't think that was allowed in the Christian walk. This was a huge turning point for me. God was using Lee to come along side me and strengthen my walk with the Lord. It wasn't long before Lee and Barbara became family with the Davises. We shared movies, music, too much Blue Bell Ice Cream and the love of God. To say Lee was an influence in my life would be an understatement.

Soon afterwards, Lee presented to the Church the "Experiencing God" Bible study written by Henry Blackaby. This study changed my heart. It introduced me to a God who is always on the move to reach the lost, to help others and got me thinking of Him instead of being focused on me. This study led by Lee helped me and my family understand that God speaks to us if we let him. And that the relationship we have with Him is just that, a relationship. We know him, and he knows us. How do we talk to him? By simply talking to him, in prayer, in His word. The God that was introduced to me was a living, loving God. Jill says, while we were doing the

"Experiencing God" Bible study as a church, Lee also encouraged every church member to read through the Bible in a year. Each week in the church program was a list of our daily reading for the week. The combination of these two things led to our most life transforming time of spiritual growth! Amen!

Another amazing and life altering program that Pastor Lee introduced to Anchor Baptist Church was "Growing Kids God's Way," written by Gary and Anne Marie Ezzo. We met weekly with Pastor Lee and Barbara as well as two other families. Not only was it a wonderful time of fellowship as we shared a weekly meal together, the Bible based guidance we all received as young parents was invaluable in bringing up our children. Concepts we will never forget and we still use to this day with our 5 grandchildren (the interrupt rule is a lifesaver)! Another great truth we learned was emphasizing to our children who they are in Christ as well as who they are in our family. Reminding them that when they are out in their world, they represent our family and our values. We will always remember fondly and with pride an incident when we were discussing with the girls about something one of their friends had done that was inappropriate when one of them piped up and said "We're the Davises and we don't do those things!" GKGW was truly a study that absolutely altered the way we raised our children and the amazing young women and mothers they turned out to be. It is such a blessing to see them both use these same principles in their approach to raising their children.

The "Experiencing God" study, AWANA, and GKGW were so influential and as a result, many areas of our Christian walk grew. Our tithing became a regular exercise (and the Lord always supplied!). We became more involved in serving others, doing our daily Bible study and being part of the fabric of Anchor Baptist. If the Church doors were open, more than likely we were there. God has used Pastor Lee because of one thing, his faithful obedience. Saying 'yes Lord.' He walks the walk, and he talks the talk. Lee and Barbara's influence on our family is immeasurable. We are now passing down our experience from our church in Texas to our kids and grandkids in Virginia. Spiritual to practical things like operating a family budget and saving for retirement. Lee's preaching was (and still is) a pipeline of Bible based principals taught by Lee, passed on to many. We are so thankful God put the McDowells into our life. I'll leave you with one of my favorites from our Anchor Baptist Church years!

> Joshua 24:15, "But if serving the LORD seems undesirable to you, then choose for yourselves this day whom you will serve, whether the gods your ancestors served beyond the Euphrates, or the gods of the Amorites, in whose land you are living. But as for me and my household, we will serve the LORD."
>
> Brian & Jill Davis

Ira & Judy Sansom

When I became pastor at First Baptist Church Spring Branch in Houston, Texas, in September 1986, Judy Sansom was the Pastor's Secretary and church Financial Secretary. Very few secretaries have ever been as competent and have complemented the ministry of the Pastor as did Judy. Ira and Judy were a gift from God to our church. Their kids were a great compliment to their parenting. For almost 35 years we have been best of friends.

It was interesting, though, to find out that with their involvement, influence, and important positions in the church, something as basic as "giving" was a little "lacking" in their personal finances. God had a special moment for this couple as the Word of God was shared in the scant 2 years we were together. Their story is one of the most powerful testimonies of what God can do when two hearts agree with God and submit to His power to show that He is "able to do exceeding abundantly above all that we ask or think, according to the power that worketh in us" (Ephesians 3:20). Many would wish to have such a story as the Sansoms. Truth creates faithfulness.

We lived in Houston from 1976 to 1988 and were members of First Baptist Church Spring Branch. Life there was pretty good because we had fallen into a very nice and compatible young married church group. We did things together all the time, such as hunting, golfing, fishing, and especially camping. Many of us owned small campers, and we loved to camp as a group at various campgrounds, either on the Guadalupe or Frio Rivers and many times at a campground in Cleveland, Texas called Chain-O-Lakes. Life was good and comfortable for us, except we were drowning in credit card debt. Enter Lee McDowell as the new pastor at FBCSB. What a piece of work he was! Loud, brash and happy!! He loved us all with a sincerity we hadn't experienced from the previous pastor. Judy was his secretary, and I was his friend.

Then the waters began to muddy…he started a sermon series on the dreaded subject of TITHING. From my experience as a lifelong Baptist, most pastors avoided the subject except for, maybe, a yearly soft message on the subject during the annual budget planning time. Not Lee, he blasted away at the subject and made no apologies. This was just his style , and God began to convict me in a way I had never felt on the subject of tithing. I had done something I probably shouldn't have; I peeked at some of the giving records of people I knew in the church whenever Judy brought them home to stuff in envelopes for the annual giving report needed by the IRS. What I found both amazed and humbled me. I saw that some who made lots more than I did, barely gave at all, and one couple in particular whose breadwinner had been out of work for over a year continued to give at the same level they gave prior to being laid off. My heart never was the same again.

I never treated any of the people differently because I knew their giving secrets. I was, simply, convicted heavily. However, due to our considerable credit card debt, I felt like we couldn't tithe, even half of what I knew we should be giving. Back to Brother Lee, he kept pounding away at me, because I knew he was speaking specifically to me each sermon. He was even staring at me when he preached, or so I thought. So in a quiet moment, with just me and the Lord, I got the word... "you can tithe anyway, forget about the credit card debt, I've got this under control, I just need you to follow where I lead you." So Judy and I wrote our first full tithe check the next Sunday, and we have continued and never stopped.

I was ordained as a deacon, had a good job, company car, and life was good. Now, I'm not going to tell you that everything went smoothly. Life happens! The credit cards still got their monthly payments, some with a little extra. But they were still there, haunting me each month. I felt so foolish, because I had followed the world's chief liar, Satan, into a pit of debt that seemed insurmountable. So we moved forward by faith, trusting in the Lord and hoping to figure out how to get rid of the debt by ourselves.

The Lord had another way to handle it (remember, He told me that He had it all under control). I got laid off, right before Christmas 1987. I found another job within a couple of weeks, but the job was in Dallas. I left Houston for Dallas early each Monday morning, drove to Dallas, then returned to Houston on Friday afternoon. Meanwhile, we put our little Houston home up for sale. Guess what, no buyers for 6 months, except for one man who wanted to steal the house from us. We decided we would try to rent the house and rent somewhere in the Dallas area. Again, the Lord had a better idea. The week after we pulled our little house off the market, one of our neighbors contacted us and said his parents wanted to relocate from Pasadena to our old neighborhood so they could be closer to grandkids. They offered us exactly what we were asking for the house, and the deal was done! We found a nice home in Wylie, Texas that was priced way below market because it was a HUD repo. The price, exactly what we could afford.

Back to those pesky credit cards, we took the extra money we got for our home in Houston, above what we put down for the new home loan in Wylie, and paid off all our credit cards and a car loan for a new Suburban we had purchased not long before I was laid off. We sat down in our bedroom, on the floor, and cut up every credit card into tiny little pieces.

The Lord wasn't through with us yet. We had become very active at First Baptist Church in Wylie. I agreed to teach a married couples Bible study and Judy was working for the Baptist General Convention of Texas as the assistant to the Youth Evangelist Director, part of the Evangelism Division of the BGCT. Our pastor came

146

to me one day and asked if I would give a tithing testimony, because I'm sure he knew us to be regular tithers. I'm a firm believer in giving an answer right now to any question posed to me, especially in church. With my wife working as a pastor's secretary and then as an employee of the convention, I had come to recognize what I called the "Baptist no," otherwise known as the statement, "Let me pray about it." Not me, I already knew the answer and I would give it, yes or no. I said yes and decided to let the Lord guide me as to what I would say. The time came for me to give the tithing testimony. I got up before the entire congregation on Sunday morning and blabbed away, no notes, just me and my bigmouth, chasing all kinds of rabbit trails with my testimony, but telling exactly how my mind was whirling around whenever I was listening to Brother Lee's messages and lessons on tithing.

I left the pulpit exhausted and had amnesia as to what I had actually said. I'm pretty sure there was lots of laughter, but I didn't tell any jokes. It was just me being me up in front of a bunch of people I loved and respected. The next Sunday the pastor pulled me aside and told me that a family was convicted from my testimony and had written the church a check for $50,000. I was completely blown away. Surely, nothing I said was good enough to get that kind of response. Hello Lord, how did You take my words and make them have such an impression on someone. I'll never understand. Turns out, that family were friends we knew from our Bible Study group. I'm going to summarize some of the things that happened in the next few years. I was laid off 3 more times and the Lord was faithful and kept me in work and funds so that we lacked for nothing. Our oldest son suffered a diving accident and became a quadriplegic, paralyzed from his shoulders down.

Again, the Lord was faithful because the friend that was convicted from my testimony was our son's Bible Study teacher. That family came to us and gave us a check for $10,000 to help with an addition to our home to accommodate our son's disability. Other church members followed their lead and donated materials or labor to the project and that $10,000 was enough to complete the job. We never wanted for anything because the Lord was faithful. Later, that same family was able to purchase some land in Miami, Oklahoma and used the funds from a business that they sold to construct a church camp. We were invited to the grand opening, which we attended, and that gentleman came to me, privately, and told me that this was "all your fault." My crazy testimony was still convicting him.

In 2002, Judy was contacted by a gentleman we knew from some of the BGCT events she arranged and invited her to come and consider being his executive assistant at the Highland Lakes Baptist Encampment. Housing would be provided along with all utilities and health insurance for our family. I was employed by a major insurance company at the time, knocking down 6 figures. After we visited the campus, just outside of Austin, Texas, the Lord's conviction came upon both of us. We sold our home in Wylie, we quit our jobs, and we "came to camp". There wasn't a job for me *in that ministry, so I was able to get on with a local insurance firm, but only for about 11 months, until I was, again, laid off. The Lord, once again, showed Himself faithful. At just the time I needed it, a position became available in the Highland Lakes ministry and I'm part of that ministry today. I'm haunted and humbled to this very day about how all these events unfolded. But ultimately, Brother Lee, this was ALL YOUR FAULT!! I learned a valuable life lesson from you, the Lord can change your "wanter" to what it should be and He is always faithful.*

Ira Sansom

Brett & Lucia Westmoreland

I love divine appointments, don't you? I mean those "coming togethers" of two or more people that God has arranged the moment, the place, the people, and all the particulars. Well that was the way it was with our meeting Brett and Lucia Westmoreland. Lucia visited our church one Sunday morning with a heart God had prepared for what she would see and hear. How she came to be at church that morning was divine in itself, the working of God to bring her there at that moment. But, the "appointment" didn't end there. It continued into the next week when Barbara and I went to the Westmoreland home. And what took place in the living room of that sweet home is a testimony of our God Who is still in the miracle business!

I will let Lucia tell their story, but let me say that it has been our joy to be associated with the Westmorelands in so many ways. Brett and I doing some home visitations, the weddings of some of our kids (both families!), and many other spiritual activities are all a part of how God has taken His Truth and moved it down from one person to another to another. Few people might know that one of Brett's grandfathers, Dr. E. H. Westmoreland, pastored one of the largest Baptist churches in Houston many years ago (1938-1971), South Main Baptist Church. God is always at work. Brett and Lucia's son, Seth, is now Children's Pastor of the First Baptist Church, Magnolia, Texas. Truth creates faithfulness.

With enough of a church history, I knew it was our responsibility (or, at least mine) to introduce God to our children. My husband, Brett, and I were married in 1979. His grandfather had pastored one of the largest Baptist churches in Houston, Texas. We never attended church as a married couple until the one I tell you about today.

I had visited several churches of different denominations and did not feel a connection. We received a flyer from a church that had started down the street from our home in the elementary school our kids attended. It seemed logical to go check out the church. God does sometimes work in mysterious ways!

On my first visit to Anchor Baptist Church, I felt welcomed immediately. Pastor Lee's message of salvation was simple and seemed attainable. It was something I'd never heard before. God spoke to my heart that morning in a way I had never experienced. Having been raised in a different denomination, the message I came away with there was that I could never be sure I could ever make it to heaven. In the message that first Sunday at Anchor, God helped me to see and hear His Truth. I wanted to know more.

I had filled out the Welcome Card for visitors, and within a couple of days the pastor and his wife, Barbara, came by our home for a visit. WOW! After some discussion, Pastor Lee mentioned that I had noted on the Welcome Card an interest in wanting to know how to become a Christian. In a few moments, we were bowing our heads in my living room, and I was praying and trusting the Lord Jesus Christ to be my personal Savior. Amen! Brett had come into the living room about the time we were going to pray. When we finished, he was in tears. God got hold of his life that day in a new way also.

Becoming a part of Anchor, and active in church life became so important to me and my family. Brett had grown up in a church like this. He became active again for the first time in years.

Anchor had a wonderful children's ministry. Having been raised only attending one type church that did not have this kind of ministry, I was pleased that my kids actually had a great time, and that they wanted to come the next Sunday also.

The Life groups were also positive for our marriage. We enjoyed the fellowship with other families which taught us how to have real friends without having to partake of alcohol.

Sunday School was new to me as well. The adult class had me searching and reading the Bible, another new experience. After we had been a part of the church for around 6 months or so, I volunteered to teach the 1st graders. The Sunday School material taught me Bible stories I'd never heard before.

Finally, the ladies ministry was another new first for me. Barbara was terrific with the subjects we studied, and I loved the arts and crafts classes. The ladies retreats were a special treat. Getting to know godly women who truly cared for others were an example for my life as a wife and mother.

As you can see, this was a church like none that I had ever been a part of, and God truly became a part of the Westmoreland family that continues these 30 years later. Brett was licensed to the Gospel Ministry by Pastor McDowell and the Anchor family also! Our son, Seth, is the children's pastor at First Baptist Magnolia (Texas).

I am not sure what path I would have taken had it not been for Anchor Baptist Church and Pastor Lee and Barbara. God worked a miracle in our lives. I've visited *other churches, and I can honestly say I first felt the peace and love of the Lord from these folks.*

Lucia Westmoreland

Randy & Jolyne White

I met Randy and Jolyne White when I became their pastor in September, 1986. A young couple without any children, very involved in our church. Three things are most memorable for me in those early years: 1) I had the privilege of ordaining Randy as a deacon of the church; 2) I had the privilege of being at the hospital with Randy as Jolyne gave birth to both of their oldest girls. The second one a little out of the ordinary (the baby, Paige, wasn't positioned right and the doctor had to earn his pay on delivering her while Randy and I and others were praying); and 3) the very first VBS (actually a Backyard Bible Club) of the new church we started in 1988...one of the "clubs" was held in the White's back yard. Randy and Jolyne lived "out west" of Houston at that time. I remember going a few times to pick up Randy to go fishing at the coast, and the rabbits were numerous in the pre-dawn hours along the road leading to their neighborhood. Not today! Houston has grown way farther west since those days.

When Randy and Jolyne moved to Mississippi a few years later, our fellowship time was gone, but the trail of Life (God's Life) that the Whites have travelled has been a huge blessing to this old pastor's heart. Their oldest daughter, Brooke, was our oldest daughter's (Kelly) flower girl in Kelly's wedding in Marshall in 1992. Barbara and I have visited the Whites on a couple of occasions over the years in their fabulous country home in Natchez. Their family has grown to 7 children and 5 grand-children. They are the epitome of a Proverbs 3:5-6 couple and home. Read with joy their recount of a couple of truths that have brought freedom to their lives all these years. Truth creates faithfulness.

Remembering back, it was the first of September, 1986, that Lee McDowell became our pastor at FBC/Spring Branch. Little did we know at that time that God would make such dramatic changes in our family's life. It wasn't long after the McDowells came to our church that we got to know them. We immediately clicked, and they became more to us than our Pastor and wife...they became like family to us. We didn't have any family that lived close to us and our girls bonded with them like they were their grandparents. They called Bro. Lee "PawPaw" and Barbara "Bro. Lee". It was the cutest thing. I think our blonde headed girls reminded them of their

150

own two daughters when they were little. We were young and naïve and they took us under their wings and taught us so many things.

But the one thing that stands out to me the most is how to be good managers of your money — which we weren't. Randy and I married when my husband was in his last year of college. We struggled to make ends meet. He went to school and I worked at an Insurance Company. We lived in the married dorms at the college and pretty much lived off Spam. When he graduated from the University of Southern Mississippi, he got a job working for Shell Oil Company in Houston, Texas, so we moved and thought we were big stuff living in a big city with a good job. We got credit cards and started charging things left and right and got into debt up to our eyeballs.

My main desire was to have lots of children and be able to stay at home with them. When Bro. Lee became pastor at FBC/Spring Branch, and preached on financial freedom and had seminars also, God began a work in our lives that is still flourishing today. We knew in order for my desire to come true, we needed to get out of debt and tear up those credit cards.

We learned to buy things on a cash basis. We were introduced to the "envelope system". This is where you have an envelope for the different items you spend money on. For example, we had a "groceries" envelope. A "clothing" envelope". There were envelopes for the bills, etc. Once that money was gone in that envelope, you were done. We had to make a budget in order for all of this to work. Before long, we were out of debt. And when my first child came along, I was able to quit work and stay home with her. We even bought our first home.

Since this time, we have had a total of 7 children and I continued to stay at home with all of them. Now that my baby is in school, I have gone back to work working in the same school she attends so I am able to be home the same hours she is. We are much older and wiser now since we first met the McDowells, and we owe much of this to the things they had taught us from God while we were under their care.

We continue to keep in touch and still feel like they are family to us. We have also continued the same financial planning all through the years and we have added 2 sons-in-law, 1 daughter-in-law and 5 grandchildren to our bunch. And we own our beautiful home — which is a blessing to not be in debt. We thank God for His Truth, and His faithfulness. And we have lived our lives for many years now "trusting God for His supply, and living on it." Philippians 4:19 is more than just some words on a page in a bible. They are Truth. "My God shall supply all your need according to His riches in glory by Christ Jesus." And God has proved them.

Jolyne White

Tom Hagen

God brought Tom and Vee Hagen into our lives in the late 70's. I hired Tom as a salesman in the boat business I was in. He was a self-described "Young Yank. Ready and willing to work." I never had been that closely involved with someone from Pennsylvania before. He was exactly as he described.

Tom was also a "learner." He listened, he grasped, he applied what we showed him about our style of sales. And he was dependable. We developed a friendship, as well as being co-workers.

When I left the boat business, I was still in contact with Tom. And when I became a Christian, he was one of the first with whom I began to share my new-found faith. I still remember the joy in my heart when Christ broke through to Tom. It was a couple of years later that he and Vee and their kids moved back to Bedford, PA. And God had a major event planned for them that dramatically altered their lives. Listen to Tom give an account of his story of his Savior, Jesus Christ, and the guidance and impact in Tom's life. And see if you can relate to God's revelation of JPS to Tom. Truth creates faithfulness.

Jesus Christ came into my life in 1981. I trusted Him to be my Savior at Sagemont Baptist Church, Houston, TX. I had first known Lee McDowell while a salesman in the boat business. I was salesman at the store he managed. After Lee left the company and later became a Christian, he began to tell me how that had happened and shared the Gospel with me. I trusted Christ to be my Savior in just a short period of time from Lee's initial witnessing.

For the past 37 years I have had multiple opportunities to learn more about Christ, Christianity, and life as a Christian. Each time God has shown me more of His Truth that impacted my life. But recently, while interacting with McDowell more often, we began discussing how God is a part of everything I do, and has been all these years. Proverbs 3:5-6, "Trust in the LORD with all thine heart; lean not unto thine own understanding. In all thy ways acknowledge Him, and He shall direct thy paths", became a verse that I wanted to know more about and understand its impact on my life.

Sixteen years ago I had an accident at a business I owned. I fell off a tall ladder replacing a light on a pole in the lot. It dramatically changed my health. I lost my mobility, my wife of 30 years, and everything I had worked for. My body was broken, my heart was broke, and my bank account was broke. The only thing that wasn't broke was my faith in Christ. Looking back, yes it was very tough, but I can honestly say that today, I am more happy and at peace than I ever dreamed I could ever be. Only Christ could have made it happen.

I will never forget the time during my divorce while I was in a private room waiting for my turn in front of the judge, I took off my jacket and was on my knees praying. I didn't know at the time the room had a security camera, and all of a sudden two security officials came in and wanted to know what I was doing on the floor. I told them I was talking to Christ. They searched me and my brief case, and as they left one guard asked me if I thought prayers work. I told him if not for Christ I would already be dead. He shook my hand and asked me to pray for him! Ha! Go figure that out! JPS at work before I even knew about it! (more on that in a bit).

As the McDowells and I have discussed God's Word over and over, I began to see how God's direction in my life affected my thoughts, my decisions, my actions, and my interactions with others. Life as a Christian became more than just getting up in the morning, saying hello or talking about things with others, or me making decisions that I thought would give me a better life. Christ in me was becoming more and more like He was alive and real and actually in charge of my life.

I really began to focus and think more on what it really meant to trust God. I began to know what it meant to not lean on my understanding, but lean on God's. And I began to confess that God was controlling me more than I had ever known or acknowledged. And then I began to see how God really was directing my paths, bringing folks into my life at a particular time for a very particular reason, and putting me in a particular spot at a particular time to accomplish a particular purpose. It was crazy!

What's more, I began to tell people that it was Jesus Christ who brought it all to pass. I began to tell people that it was Jesus Christ who had done what had taken place. So many people thought I was weird, or crazy. Ha!

With all my many medical issues the last 15 years, I have been to many doctors. Many have said to me, "Tom, how can you have all these things happen to you and have to deal with all this, and you seem so peaceful, so calm?" I look them in the face and say, "Jesus." They spook out! I have family that don't have much to do with me any more.

Lee and I had gotten more specific about the impact of Proverbs 3:5-6 for a few weeks, and one night it is snowing. At 2am I am on my front porch with my dog, Frank. I am sweeping snow off the porch, then on my sidewalk. There is 22 inches of snow. It is silent. No one around. It is a beautiful sky. Beautiful snowfall. There is no wind blowing. I had walked about 100 yards or so from my front door. Then, at the moment, I thought, "Where am I?" The thought came to my mind about how the world uses a GPS to find a particular spot, determine where someone is, or designate a place on a map. And out of the blue, God brought this thought to mind: JPS. Jesus Positioning System. I freaked out! Jesus knows where I am. He can direct me back to my front door. He will get me home. JPS – It's where I am at with Christ.

Jesus does this very thing both physically and spiritually with us! He positions us. He positions others in our path at a particular time for a particular purpose or reason. Get out! Are you serious?!? (that's an old Pennsylvania slang for an exclamation, excitement, or wonder). Thank You, Jesus Christ!

153

One day I am talking to my postman. I was questioning him about the pedometer he was wearing on his arm. After figuring how much he walks each day and how much that would be in one year, I told him he could walk across the United States in one year. It is about the same distance as he walks his route in one year! And then I mentioned JPS to him, and that Jesus would have him in the right place with the right people all the time! We rejoiced together in that.

A couple of months later I am talking to a friend who owns a nursery (Bill Greenwalt, Greenwalt's Nursery). He loves Jesus. I began to tell him about JPS. Just today he came to plant a couple of bushes and put out bark mulch in my plant beds. He says out of the blue, "Tom, you know that JPS stuff you were telling me about a while back? A 70 yr. old neighbor of mine, he's up in northern Pennsylvania cutting trees by himself out in the middle of nowhere. A large limb broke and fell on him. He is laying on his back, limb across his chest, fumbles around and gets his phone. Trouble is…he is in an area with NO cell service. He couldn't dial 911, the phone wouldn't work. He had his daughter's phone number in his phone where he could punch 1 number and it would dial her. Lo, and behold, the call went through! JPS! His daughter calls authorities, and they find him, and life-flight him to the hospital. Christ saved his life! He is still in the hospital. The doctors told him he would be paralyzed, but today he is moving his toes and 1 leg…JPS!"

Ever since my life's path took me to Texas, to getting a job selling boats with Lee McDowell, to trusting Jesus Christ as my Savior, He has led me down paths that I would have never taken without His directing. I just didn't realize and recognize it until JPS! Thank You, Jesus Christ!

One thing is interesting. Even when some really bad things have happened in my life, I never lost my faith in Christ. But just recently, God showed me that it was Him in control, directing my paths all the time. I now think of only trusting Him in all things, forgetting about trusting my understanding of things, and proclaiming Him in ALL things! Thank You, Jesus Christ!

Jesus Christ has given me a joy and a testimonial to tell more and more people about how He does exactly what He says He will do in Proverbs 3:5-6. I want to be found faithful to tell as many as I possibly can. Jesus is Truth. He makes us free from any bondage this world has held us captive to. He will move heaven and earth, if necessary, to get us into position to free us from any bondage.

Christ has fixed, and continues to fix, all the years of pain – mentally, physically, and financially. One day I'll thank Him in person!

Tom Hagen

Truth is not only preached but demonstrated. Words can be meaningless without a testimony of personal application. Truth demonstrated creates faithfulness, because where Truth is, the Lord is. And only He can create. And create He does through His Truth!

> *"Lord Jesus, thank You for Your gift of seeing Faithful Ones practice and share Your Truth in their lives, and the lives of those they have touched...Truth that was shared with me, and in turn was shared with them. 2 Timothy 2:2 is a huge Truth for all of Christianity to share in Your plan for giving forward what You have given in the first place. May the world be full of Faithful Ones!"*

Oh yes, I pray that God gives you some Faithful Ones to forward some God-given Truth! And, remember this, Truth will always find a way!

Chapter Seventeen

A Personal Note
"I don't HAVE TO. I GET TO! And I WANT TO!"

"Therefore if any man be in Christ, he is a new creature: old
things are passed away; behold, all things are become new."
2 Corinthians 5:17

Everything you have read so far has had an important impact on my
life. Each Truth has changed me. These are foundational Truths, those
critical undergirdings of my character, my decisions, and my actions. May
I encourage you likewise to make decisions...from foundational
Truths...that will make other decisions for you.

I bring this writing to a close by first travelling back to Pastor John
Morgan's office at Sagemont Baptist Church, May 20, 1980, and thinking
about that first verse of scripture that he gave to Barbara and me right
after we as sinners prayed to ask God for His forgiveness, cleansing, and
to put our trust in the Lord Jesus Christ as our very own personal Savior,
and became Saints: 2 Corinthians 5:17. Born Again. Old things had
passed away. All things had become new. We were "in Christ" from that
moment on. We were a New Creature, a work of God (remember, ONLY
GOD can "create"). The "old man" was crucified and gone.

But, in addition, as it was to be revealed fully to me about 15 years
later, Christ was Living in us! That is when the seagulls gather in huge
numbers and start squawking and circling and diving! Food, spiritual
food, is on the TABLE!

And then sometime later, in the days that followed our New Birth,
something huge dawned on me: I realized that:

- because of my new birth into the Family of God, and God giving
  His Holy Spirit (Himself) to indwell me, and

- because of God's Soul living in me I possess His mind, His
  emotions, and His will, and

- because of a choice I can make, I can Live with Jesus' Spirit and
  Soul in control.

I do not HAVE TO live life as a Christian. I GET TO Live Life (actually His Life) as a Christian. And, then in later years, my focus was turned to HIS DOING THE LIVING!

Every moment of every day became a life of choices. And I began to choose LIFE. I first had begun to dwell on WHO I AM IN CHRIST. Then, several years later, I began dwelling on WHO CHRIST IS IN ME. Wow! The Truths are phenomenal. Let me give you some that I think about over and over: (I give you just a few with Bible verses. The work is up to you to discover from God's Word the other great "belongings" that are yours as a Christian!)

Who I Am IN CHRIST

- I am God's child for I am Born Again of the incorruptible seed of the Word of God which liveth and abideth forever – 1 Peter 1:23

- I am forgiven of all my sins, having been washed in Christ's Blood – Ephesians 1:7; Hebrews 9:14; Colossians 1:14; 1 John 1:9, 2:12

- I am a new creation of God – 2 Corinthians 5:17

- I am one of God's Saints – Romans 1:7; 1 Corinthians 1:2; Philippians 1:1

- I am holy and without blame before God – Ephesians 1:4

- I am more than a conqueror – Romans 8:37

- I am a joint-heir with Jesus – Romans 8:17

- (the list goes on & on. I have one list of 70 such biblical Truths!)

Who CHRIST Is IN ME

- Christ is my Shepherd – Psalm 23; John 10:1-18

- Christ is my peace – John 14:27

- Christ is my joy – John 15:9-11

- Christ is my love – John 15:9-10

- Christ is my faith – Galatians 5:22

- Christ is my righteousness – 2 Corinthians 5:21

- Christ is my righteous mind – 1 Corinthians 2:16

- Christ is my guarantee of eternal life – Ephesians 1:13-14
- (the list goes on & on. I am sure this list has no end…)

Now listen, as a Christian, you should make it an imperative to search the Holy Scriptures on an ongoing basis to make your own list of ALL the Truth that God has given you about who you are IN CHRIST, and Who CHRIST is IN YOU! Do not neglect to do this! It is vitally important to know just who you are as a Born Again Believer, AND to discover and appropriate all that Christ is for you. These two realms will make your Life as a Christian totally different from what you have been living!

Before I go any further, let me emphasize the Truth of 2 Corinthians 5:17 and, "old things are passed away; behold, all things are become new." It is critically important to get it correct JUST what has "passed away" and what has "become new." This verse is all about the spiritual changes God has made in a Born Again Believer (New Creation) and not the "physical" changes (from the acts and ways and thinking of the Old Man). Far too many think that all the "old ways" have to pass, and all your "new ways" are to be godly and righteous. Many go so far as to say, "Well, I thought (Bill) got saved, but he must not have…he still (drinks)." Now listen carefully: even though the New Life does CHANGE many things, that is NOT the epitome of the New Birth. The New Birth is a New Creation, resulting in Believers having the "old Adamic spirit" removed, Christ's Spirit (Holy Spirit) "put in," AND Christ's Soul (His Mind, His Emotions, and His Will) "put in." And, our "old Adamic soul" still remains. Believers here on Earth have two (2) souls- hence "double-souled." It is between the two souls that our "battle" is fought. THAT is what has "passed away" and "become new" and "still remains." Knowing this, and getting it correct, will lead to a clear, concise, and correct "picture" and understanding of "WHO WE ARE IN CHRIST," and "WHO HE IS IN US," and WHAT is battling HIM in us.

It is interesting that teaching and preaching in this day leave little room for "growing in Christ" or for "carnal Christians." It is also interesting that those most critical of New Believers are chock full of "sins" that they never want to address of themselves.

I mention coming to the realization of the indwelling of the Holy Spirit. I remember hearing Romans 8:11 for the first time…

> "But if the Spirit of Him that raised up Jesus from the dead dwell in you, He that raised up Christ from the dead shall also quicken your mortal bodies by His Spirit that dwelleth in you."

158

The phenomenal Truth and power in those words almost blew my mind way back in 1980. The Spirit of God, God Himself, raised up Jesus from the dead. HE LIVES IN ME! He is IN ME to "quicken" MY mortal body. Just the fact of that means so much. But, the impact of the extension of His indwelling is so much more. His peace, His mind, His emotions, His will…ALL of His GIFTS, are for me.

So, for a final personal note, let me share **3 thoughts** that always guide me:

1. **"When in doubt, throw it out!"** This theme in my life oversees a whole lot of issues. It is one of those decisions that makes other decisions for me. It is interesting how I first came to this position.

Back in Baytown, Texas, while in high school in 1961-1963, one afternoon as I was making my way to a car to go to the golf course (being on the golf team), some teammates and I got to the car out near the tennis courts at Robert E. Lee High School where some of our buddies who were on the tennis team (Bill Marshall and Joel Lawless among them) were practicing. Somehow a discussion came up with those tennis guys as to how they called a shot to be inbounds or out-of-bounds when it was "close," seeing as they had no independent official. They quickly said, "The player nearest the ball makes the call. And, when in doubt, they call it out." We laughed and went on our way to the golf course. My teammates on the golf team (Mickey Reilly, Danny Tolleson, and Tommy King) and I never were confronted with that sort of "call" in golf. But that became a running joke amongst all of us for the whole time we were in school.

I don't think it was until just after Barbara and I were Born Again in 1980 that the thought of "when in doubt, call it out" ever came up again. But, out of nowhere, the issue of what to do with certain things in our house and in our lives once we became Christians was then a very important question. And "when in doubt, **throw** it out" became our mantra.

I didn't realize it particularly at the moment of salvation, but one thing that really happened was this: Barbara and I "threw out" 30+ years of religious teaching, and started what has been truthfully "a new Life, Christ's Life."

Within the next week or so after our New Birth, Barbara and I went through our home and started "throwing out" anything and everything that wasn't of Christ! And if there was any "doubt," guess what - OUT it went. THROW it out!

And then, invitations to go to places we used to go - OUT.

Things we used to do - OUT.

Clothes we used to wear - OUT.

Now, listen, if it was not of Jesus, we came to the point that we didn't want it. If it's not a teaching that lands at Jesus' feet, and shows me what He will do for me, I don't want it. *all i want is Jesus!* (I have a book coming out soon by that title, yes, and with a non-capitalized "i" in the title!).

My buddies out near the tennis courts - they gave me the thought that surfaced 17 years later and carried over to Living Life as a Christian. One that has had so much impact.

Now, listen, **I don't HAVE TO. I GET TO! And I WANT TO!** Christ Lives it out through me.

2. **It's not me, it's HIM.** For the first 15 or so years after being Born Again, I wanted to know and enjoy everything I could about "who I am in Christ." The list of scriptural truths about this is amazing (some shown above).

But when we first met Michael Wells at that retreat in Colorado about 20 years ago…wow! My focus was turned from ME to HIM. From "who I am in Christ" to "Who Christ is in me." As the years have gone by, I have begun to share and disciple as many as I can about this "Life" in every Christian that is not just a "religious idea" but the absolute foundation of **Life as a Christian**. I do not use the term, "the Christian life," any more. I speak of Christ's Life being my Life, Living Life as a Christian.

Before I get to the outstanding positives, let me share a heartfelt question that bears an answer. HOW could those who are God's "called" preachers and teachers not know all there is to know about "who we are in Christ" and "who Christ is in us," and not make that their prominent and imperative teaching to any and all Believers? Without which, those who proclaim to be "bible-believing Christians" still read the Scriptures and miss all the direct, unequivocal words from Holy Spirit that speak of Christ being our Life and all that He will do through us, and then go out and Live the parabolical teachings on the pages alongside God's revelation of His plan for His kids while on this earth? Matthew 13 gives us Jesus' guide to seeing, knowing, and discerning spiritual truth **versus** not being able to see, know, and discern such.

"Parabolical teaching." That's a good thought, isn't it? Jesus' disciples asked Him "why do You speak in parables?" He responded,

> "Because it is given to you to know the mysteries of the kingdom of heaven, but to them it is not given…Therefore, I speak to them in parables: because they seeing see not; and hearing they hear not, neither do they understand…For this people's heart is waxed gross, and their ears are dull of hearing, and their eyes they have closed; lest at any time they should see with their eyes, and hear with their ears, and should understand with their heart, and should be converted, and I should heal them. But blessed are your eyes, for they see: and your ears, for they hear. For verily I say unto you, That many prophets and righteous men have desired to see those things which ye see, and have not seen them; and to hear those things which ye hear, and have not heard them. HEAR YE THEREFORE…(Matthew 13:11-18)
> (CAPS my emphasis).

Jesus tells you and me who are Believers that there is some NT teaching that can ONLY be known and understood by those who have the eyes to see, ears to hear, and His Mind to understand. We can separate the words and what Unbelievers "get" from them, versus what Jesus intends for us to get. Believers see, read, hear, and understand what Unbelievers cannot. And it is HIM in us doing all that.

Back to REAL Life…Christ's Life…which is IN every Believer. Most Christians I have known think and believe, in reality, that this is for "eternal life" only. That His indwelling in us somehow will be the "catalyst" that takes us to Heaven when we die. And it will. BUT, they never see, or accept, His Life for NOW, here on earth while still in this physical life. They never see or acknowledge that we are two people: one that is physical, and one that is spiritual. They never abandon to the Truth of His Life IS our life. And "our life" is His Life.

This is dramatically important for EVERY Christian: the REAL "me" is HIM. The REAL "you" is HIM. The "old I" has been crucified, dead. But there is Life NOW in our earthsuit. How? Who? It is CHRIST. HE is the REAL "you" and "me" since our New Birth, that New Creation He created. Believe it. Believe Him. And enjoy Him being "you"!

Many want to give God "glory" for what He has done, but actually are thinking they "did" it. That they did it, just "in His power." IF they even acknowledge "His power." So they face each day and each instant with a fear or phobia that failure is imminent due to this thought prevalent in their minds: "after all, I am just human." Wrong! No Christian is "just human." That is a lie from the pits of hell.

When God revealed that inside my fleshly body (my earthsuit) is His Life, and by His grace (which is HIM "doing" it, whatever it is) the Life that looks like ME is not really ME, but HIM - I just about had a fanatical fit! Hallelujah! An abandonment to Him gives Him this body (earthsuit) to Live through. A choice to move back into the "flesh" takes that back, and "my old natural self" comes forth. So, each moment is a choice of mine for it either to be ME, or HIM. No matter the situation, no matter the participants, no matter the issues, it is a CHOICE.

So, I start each day with a simple choice: "Lord, I don't want any part of my old self to live through this earthsuit. I want Your Life to Live through this earthsuit. Amen." Just a choice. A choice that I GET to make.

But now, listen, **I don't HAVE TO. I GET TO! And I WANT TO!** Christ lives it out through me.

3. **Trust...Relax...Watch...Enjoy.** This theme became a part of my life when some time years ago the Lord led me to the following passages:
    "For who hath known the mind of the Lord, that he may instruct him? But we have the mind of Christ."
    1 Corinthians 2:16
    "Let this mind be in you, which was also in Christ Jesus."
    Philippians 2:5
    "Trust in the LORD with all thine heart, and lean not unto thine own understanding. In all thy ways acknowl-edge Him, and He shall direct thy paths."
    Proverbs 3:5-6

These truly have become some of the most prominent and domineering verses in my Life as a Christian. Soak on these verses, meditate long and let the Mind of the Lord speak to your heart about the implications these have for you day in and day out.

Can you grasp the power of thought, knowledge, understanding, and applicational wisdom God has granted to you and me as one of His Saints? HIS MIND. HIS TOTAL DIRECTION OF OUR LIVES. HIS EMOTIONS and HIS DECISION MAKER FOR US.

I don't know about you, but I love the simplicity and uncomplicatedness of these verses. First, God tells us through the Apostle

Paul that "we have the mind of Christ." Do you really believe that? Have you ever begun to reckon that? Appropriate that?

Now stop and think a bit on Solomon's words. And keep in mind that even though God tells us Solomon was the wisest person God has ever known, Solomon was without the New Life which includes God's Spirit and God's Soul (God's Mind, God's Emotions, God's Will). He was living out of the fleshly mind that was equipped by God to have tremendous knowledge and understanding. But WE have God's Spirit and God's Soul. How much more can I **Trust** in the LORD God with my all, making sure to not lean on any of mine own "natural" understandings, and in all my ways acknowledge Him (it is then HIM, not ME), **then Relax, Watch, and Enjoy** how and what HE DOES to direct my paths (and all that comes to me in those paths). Hooooooooooo-boy!

One of the most amazing things that is a part of my life is this: I have never made an initial contact to apply for a job. Never in my entire life. I am now 73 years of age, and every "job" I have ever had since my first one (working at a putt-putt golf course in Baytown, Texas around 10 or 11 years old) to the last church I preached at, someone else has made the "first contact" asking me to consider a position. I think back and see God's hand in each one. I have grown by seeing His hand work to be in a position today of not being concerned about "who, what, where" the next place might be - just knowing that God knows who I am, where I am, and what He wants to do through me. Life like that is as comfortable as can be.

Now, listen, just as **I don't HAVE TO. I GET TO! And I WANT TO!** Christ lives it out through me.

It can be the same for you! HE wants you to enjoy that! HIS TRUTH is as much for you as it is for me or any other Believer.

Just as I decided **"When in doubt, throw it out!"** - it can be the same for you! He wants that. HIS TRUTH is as much for you as it is for me or any other Believer.

Just as **it's not me, it's HIM** - it can be the same for you! He wants to be Him through you! Acknowledge Him. Let Him. HIS TRUTH is as much for you as it is for me or any other Believer.

Just as I **trust, relax, watch, and enjoy** - it can be the same for you! Try it. Prove it. Prove HIM. He wants you to trust Him. HIS TRUTH is as much for you as it is for me or any other Believer.

My hope and prayer is that YOU are ready for ALL of HIS TRUTH to become a part of your life each and every day.

"Lord Jesus, YOU and TRUTH are One and the Same. You have already given us ALL of Yourself, and all of Your Truth. Please REVEAL Your Truth and Yourself as You know we are ready for it.
Thank You that You will."

Oh yes, I hope and pray GOD comes with HIS TRUTH to you at just the right moment that you have a need for it. And remember this... TRUTH will always find a way!

On Being Born Again

Our Lord Jesus Christ made some very definitive statements about becoming a Christian and "gaining" Eternal Life. Read these verses carefully, and if you need further explanation or answers to some questions please contact me or someone you know who can give you God's wisdom and answers:

> "…I am the way, the truth, and the life: no man cometh unto the Father, but by Me." John 14:6

> "…I say unto thee, Except a man be born again, he cannot see the kingdom of God…That which is born of the flesh is flesh; and that which is born of the Spirit is spirit. Marvel not that I said unto thee, Ye must be born again." John 3:3, 6-7

> "He came unto His own, and His own received Him not. But as many as received Him, to them gave He power to become the sons of God, even to them that believe on His name." John 1:11-12

Within these words are the "way" of salvation. Jesus clearly is the Way. Many other scriptures lead the way to Eternal Life (Jesus) also. Everyone will die the physical death, and then face the judgment of God.

Some people call this salvation being "saved." There is truth in that, but I like to make it plain, clear, and complete that a New Birth better describes becoming a Christian and "knowing" you have become one.

Basically, anyone who has not been Born Again thinks the way to Heaven is a path of "good works." However, God's standard is perfection. Jesus Himself was perfect. And God says:

> "But as He which hath called you is holy, so be ye holy in all manner of conversation (behavior); Because it is written, Be ye holy; for I am holy." 1 Peter 1:15-16

Are you perfect? Are you holy? Do you live up to that? Well, we all know the truth is that us living a perfect life is impossible. But God sent His perfect Son to be our perfect substitutionary, all-sufficient atoning sacrifice for our sin at His Cross of Calvary. Our full forgiveness of our sin can only come through our confessing we are sinners, asking God for

His forgiveness, receiving His grace (His payment) by trusting in Him and His death and shedding of His blood for that perfect sacrifice for our sin.

Good works do matter for a Christian, but only after salvation, not to escape God's righteous judgment.

Is there a perfect prayer to pray for God's forgiveness? No. But God knows a repentant heart and a sinner's desire for His forgiveness. Yet, we have many scriptures that give us direction as to a "good" prayer for asking God's forgiveness. The following will help you if that is your desire:

Dear Lord Jesus Christ, I thank You for dying upon Your Cross for me, a guilty sinner, paying the penalty for my sin. I believe You are the way, the truth, and the life. And there is no other. I trust, and accept, and receive You gladly, as my Savior. Thank You for cleansing me and forgiving me of all my sin – past, present, and future. I believe, and by Your Holy Spirit now living in me, KNOW I am redeemed, and You will never leave me nor forsake me. You are Christ my Savior, my Lord, my God, my Life – forever! Amen.

Just as you are saved by God's grace when you trust in Christ and His payment, you are kept by God's grace for all eternity. Enjoy God's mercy, His love, His grace for all eternity as a Born Again child of God, one who WAS a sinner but is now an HOLY Saint.

B. Lee McDowell
Lee McDowell Christian Ministries
P.O. Box 633244, Nacogdoches, Texas 75963
936-645-9091
leemccm.wixsite.com/lmcm

Books To Come by
B. Lee McDowell

Dowadad Press, Publisher
A division of Lee McDowell Christian Ministries, Inc.
P. O. Box 633244, Nacogdoches, TX, 75963

all i want is Jesus! – Vol. 1
His Love, His Grace, His Sound Mind, His Shepherding

all i want is Jesus! – Vol. 2
His Faith, His Hope, His Joy, His Peace

all i want is Jesus! – Vol. 3
His Forgiveness, His Acceptance, His Presence, His Mercy

Grandpa's Goodies for His Grandkids - Vol. 1
God's Wisdom and Grace passed from one generation to another

Grandpa's Goodies for His Grandkids - Vol. 2
MORE of God's Wisdom and Grace passed from one generation
to another

Growing in God's Grace
more than the mysterious "unmerited favor"

Living In Christ's Pasture
a LIFE of peace, protection, and plenitude

The Images of God & Man
the seven trichotomies in diagrams

The Math of Life
experiencing the Life of Christ in your personal finances

Made in the USA
Columbia, SC
11 August 2021